Bloody Terrified

Bloody Terrified

The true story of a Pathfinder Crew in the RAF's 608 Squadron during WWII

Ian Redmond

Ian Redmond

In an earlier edition of this book, a story on page 224 gave the impression that Colin was involved in black market activities. This was not the case and the story has been updated to correct that impression.

Bloody Terrified
Copyright © 2020 by Ian Redmond.

ISBN: 9798559720975
Imprint: Independently published

All rights reserved.
No part of this book may be reproduced or transmitted in any form by any means without permission in writing from the author, except by a reviewer, who may quote brief passages in a review.

Title: *Bloody Terrified, The true story of a Pathfinder Crew in the RAF's 608 Squadron During WWII*

Author: Ian Redmond

Cover Design: Bob Coady

This book is dedicated to the extraordinary men and women of Bomber Command whose determination and sacrifice made a significant contribution to the final victory. Your efforts will not be forgotten.

To Colin and Doug for doing their part and finding their way home.

Ian Redmond

Introduction

During the Second World War, my father, Douglas Redmond, was a navigator on a two-man Mosquito bomber. Together with his pilot, he flew 50 sorties into Germany in late 1944 and early 1945. Although a member of the Royal Canadian Air Force, he found himself flying in a Royal Air Force Pathfinders squadron based in northeastern England.

Like many veterans, he locked his wartime memories away when he returned to civilian life, bringing back only a few reminders of his time in the services. In the early 1960s, when I was a young child, I fondly remember the times when he would come into my room at night and tell me stories about his experiences during the war. I have vague recollections of some funny anecdotes and a few mildly scary tales, but little of substance. As I grew older, these discussions became less frequent, with the only references to the war occurring when he would don his medals and join his fellow veterans on November 11th of each year at one of the local war memorials to honour the fallen. It was during these moments that I would catch a glimpse of him casting his thoughts back to his time in England – the memories, happy and sad, seeming to wash over his face.

It was not until the late 1980s when my parents came to visit me in Edmonton, Alberta, that things changed. As my father and I sat while my mother happily shopped, he gazed into the distance and said, "You know, I trained not far from here." It was as if a dam had been breeched. Suddenly the stories began to spill forth. As an older adult, I now had a greater appreciation for the war and was able to probe into what he had been thinking during those difficult years. Over the next 20 years, I was able to tease out a few stories that provided some greater insight into his war.

When he passed away in 2008, I came into possession of his military keepsakes: his flight log, his navigation chart, his medals, and buttons and brevets from his uniform. When viewed together, they provide a glimpse into a time and a place about which many members of my family have very little knowledge. It is for them that I vowed to piece the stories together and preserve my father's memory for his children, grandchildren and future generations.

As I pored over the log book, I soon realized there were large gaps in my knowledge of his time in the RAF. I was able to bridge some of these through access to material from military archives and other sources of information. The one piece of information that jumped out from all my research was the fact that he had flown his entire operational career with just one man, Colin Bell, an Englishman with whom he had briefly reconnected via e-mail in the early 2000s. Armed with this name, I began my search for any information that related to the two men and their time in the RAF. To my amazement, not only did I find records of their missions together, but I learned that Mr. Bell continues to be an active speaker in England on his experiences in the war. During the summer of 2019, I reached out to him to explain who I was and what I was doing, to which he quickly responded with a generous offer to visit with him to talk about my father and their experiences during the war.

In October 2019, I travelled to England to spend five days with the man who shared fifty bombing missions over Germany with my father. What follows is their story. While the events are factual, I have taken some licence with the dialogue in hopes of capturing the tone and nature of the conversations of that time and the personalities of the participants.

Ian Redmond

Prologue

At the outset of the Second World War, Bomber Command was a small and relatively ineffective group that relied on slow, antiquated aircraft with a limited capacity to inflict meaningful damage on an enemy that was rapidly insinuating itself across Europe. In September 1939, the Royal Air Force (RAF) boasted 33 operational bomber squadrons. Ten of these were equipped with single-engine Fairey Battles, nicknamed the "flying coffin" by aircrews because of their sluggish airspeed and an armament of only a single Vickers machine gun. Six squadrons were comprised of twin-engine Blenheim bombers which had limited range and did not have the capacity to carry substantial bomb loads. As a result, their usage was largely focussed on supporting the Allied ground forces in France, where both types of planes suffered catastrophic losses owing to their extreme vulnerability to the faster German fighters.

The remaining 17 squadrons formed the basis for the strategic bombing offensive. It was these squadrons of the early bombers, the four-engine Stirling, and the two-engine Hampden, Whitley and Wellington, that made the initial strategic forays against the Germans. The first operations saw Bomber Command focussing on military targets such as German warships and enemy airfields. Such targets were indisputably military in nature and did not require deep penetration into German territories. Raids at this stage of the war were carried out in daylight, with night flying used only as a means of dropping leaflets over occupied territories, as the ability to accurately bomb at night was not fully realized. At the outset of the war, night navigation required measurements based on the positions of the stars, combined with the concept of "dead reckoning" navigation that was based on compass, airspeed, and wind directions and speeds.

And yet, Bomber Command was dedicated to the principle of taking the war to its enemies. Day after day, for weeks on end, the RAF bombers relentlessly took the fight to the Germans. The twin-engine bombers continued to engage targets across Europe, with the early aircrews suffering tremendously in the process. Not only were they being preyed upon by the Luftwaffe, they were also dealing with the effects of flying in aircraft that provided little comfort against the frigid temperatures in the air stream. For many men, battling frostbite was a constant distraction during the long sorties against German targets. For the early planes like the Hampdens, a mission against a location like Stettin, northeast of Berlin, would take 14 hours - a long time to be subjected to the elements during a cold winter.

Initial tactics called for massed flights of the slow-moving bombers defended only by the multiple guns that could be brought to bear by flying in close formation. The concept of the fighter escort was in limited use. Indeed, it is not surprising to find that the RAF was less inclined to send its precious fighters out to do battle with a German foe that was at the peak of its powers and able to put up significant numbers of planes to engage whatever the British brought into play. Perhaps even more important, there was little desire to provoke the Germans into focussing their superior number of aircraft against targets in England as there was considerable fear that the Luftwaffe would be able to deliver a knockout blow from the air. As a result, the RAF preferred to build up the number of available aircrews in anticipation of newer and better aircraft.

During these early months, Bomber Command's efforts could best be described as an annoyance to enemy operations. As the war progressed, Bomber Command losses continued to be quite heavy, as harsh lessons were learned about the inability of a massed flight of bombers to defend themselves solely with their own limited firepower; these lessons would influence the future course of the strategic air offensive. On two occasions in late 1939, a strike force of Wellington bombers suffered fifty percent casualties, an outcome that solidified the view within Bomber Command that a heavy bomber raid in daylight could not survive in the face of interceptor fighters. By contrast, Whitley bombers flying at night all over Germany to drop leaflets suffered few losses. In this context, the move to night operations seemed inevitable.

By 1940, the RAF had begun a night-time bombing campaign that focussed on industrial targets, with an emphasis on synthetic oil production facilities. While results were initially reported as good and aircraft losses were low, aerial surveillance often showed limited damage to targeted areas. Clearly identifying individual targets in the dark required significant work. It was common in the early years of the war for bombers relying on dead reckoning navigation to miss their targets entirely. Surveys of bombing photographs and other sources published during August 1941 indicated that fewer than one bomb in ten fell within 5 miles (8.0 km) of its intended target. Thusly, one of the most urgent problems facing Bomber Command was the development of reliable and accurate navigational aids to improve the success of night raids. Given the destructive power of the German air force, Bomber Command was not prepared to return to heavy bombing in daylight. Even with the increased focus on flying at night, the advent of improved German defenses - night fighters and anti-aircraft guns linked to radar - had seen Bomber Command losses continue to grow as the calendar turned to 1941.

In 1942, two things happened that made major changes to the bombing strategy. The first was the appointment of Air Chief Marshal Sir Arthur Harris, known as "Bomber" Harris, to lead Bomber Command. The second was the introduction to the British air force arsenal of powerful four-engine Stirlings, Halifaxes and Lancasters. These planes, with their increased payload capacity, greater range and electronic navigational equipment provided the means to change the plan of attack. The RAF now had the ability to deploy new tactics designed to overwhelm German defences, one of which was the creation of a new group tasked with marking the targets for the main body of bombers. With the advent of this special force, who were christened the Pathfinders, the crews of the main body of bombers were relieved of this responsibility, which led directly to higher success rates that had previously eluded the determined RAF crews.

Equally important to the change in Bomber Command's fortunes was the strength of leadership and forceful character of their new commanding officer. Recognizing the potential of the larger aircraft now available to the RAF to heighten Bomber Command's striking capacity, Harris changed the direction of the bombing offensive by shifting the focus to targeting whole cities in an effort to destroy both the factories and their workers, while at the same time attempting to diminish German morale and the will of the population to continue the fight.

Beginning in June 1942, with only about one eighth of the number of planes that would eventually become available, Bomber Command inflicted enough damage that Germany had to divert people and resources to repair targeted areas. By the end of the year, operating with 25 per cent of its eventual capacity, Bomber Command's actions against factories had begun to show tangible results. Apart from the direct impacts on the targeted facilities, bombing had resulted in the reallocation of large calibre guns from the Russian front to scattered locations and cities across the Reich to defend against air attacks. Equally important, in the eyes of Bomber Harris, was the decrease in the production of German heavy tanks, which he estimated to be in the range of 6,000 vehicles. (Harris, 1984). The former loss was significant, as the 88 mm gun was the only one capable of penetrating the armour of the Russian heavy tanks. The reallocation of these guns from the Russian front to scattered locations was the German response to the need to address the unpredictability of where the strategic bombers would strike next. The resulting reduction in German anti-tank ability had severe consequences for the Wehrmacht's capacity to defend itself against advancing Allied armour-supported ground forces.

The Allied bomber offensive also presented the Germans with the requirement to defend every city, military installation and factory that supported the war effort. In order to do so, the Germans stationed hundreds of thousands of men across Germany to man the air defense system. Albert Speer, the German Minister of Armaments, estimated that 900,000 men who would otherwise have been available to fight were required as part of the German anti-aircraft command. This was supplemented by a further 200,000 whose skills were required to keep the regime operating, including the plumbers, electricians, and other tradesmen needed to repair bomb damage. (Harris, 1984). Taken in this context, Bomber Command's efforts throughout the war deprived the German army of well over a million men and a large portion of their anti-tank abilities, something no other branch of the Allied services could claim. In recognition of the impact, Speer wrote that the effects of the strategic bombing of Germany were underestimated, describing it as the greatest lost battle for Germany in all of the war.

By 1943, the RAF was utilizing new tactics and technology that increased the effectiveness of bombing. Added to this was the arrival of the United States Army Air Force (USAAF), an event that provided the means to commence an offensive that continued through the day and into the night. Using the combined power of the RAF and the USAAF, the Allied bomber forces began to overwhelm the Germans. In 1944, in addition to continuing to assault major German cities, bombers attacked fuel supplies, supported the invasion of western Europe by softening up coastal defences, and blocked German efforts to reinforce their armies.

At the same time, Bomber Command initiated a major naval campaign that resulted in the destruction of one third of German U-boats in their ports and the laying of 30,000 tonnes of mines in areas frequented by the submarines. In response to the effectiveness of the bombing campaign, Germany began prefabricating their submarines inland and shipping them to port for assembling, shipping that could only be done via canal. Most of these canals were ultimately destroyed by heavy bombers.

In the early years of the war, RAF Bomber Command could have been described as a small group of limited effectiveness. It is clear that the lessons learned combined with changing tactics, better aircraft, and the arrival of a forceful leader, transformed the group into an arm of the service that had an enormous capacity to wreak destruction on the enemy. As the war neared its end in 1945, Bomber Command had grown from 33 to 108 squadrons with over 1,500 aircraft. By the end of hostilities, the bombing offensive had disrupted Nazi industries, oil production, and communications and had reduced major industrial cities to ruins. When the final tally was taken at the end of the war, Bomber Command had flown 364,514 operational sorties, dropped 1,035,500 tons of bombs and lost 8,325 aircraft.

These impressive numbers must be tempered by the cost. At the height of the bomber offensive, about four percent of planes would be shot down on every raid. One might think that this meant a heavy bomber crew had a 96 percent chance of returning intact, but when one considers that such crews were expected to fly thirty such operations over a period of three months, it quickly becomes apparent that survival rates for aircrews were quite low. The actual casualty numbers bear this out. Of Bomber Command's 125,000 aircrew who took the fight into enemy occupied territories over the course of the conflict, 55,573 were killed in action, roughly 45 out of every 100 airmen who joined up. Of the remaining 55, 6 were seriously wounded and 8 became prisoners of war. In the end, only 41 out of every 100 men were physically unharmed, although the number that suffered what is now termed post-traumatic stress disorder (PTSD) likely reduces these numbers to an unknown degree.

As alarming as these final numbers are, at the beginning of the war the Bomber Command survival rate was only 10 percent, increasing progressively until the end of the war. Throughout the war, the aircrews faced formidable odds that were seldom appreciated outside of the RAF. During the great air offensives of 1943 and 1944, the short-term statistics foretold that fewer than 25 out of each 100 crews would survive their first tour of 30 operations. Yet the crews buckled on their chutes and set out with unshakeable resolution night after night. They fell prey to the hazards of icing, lightning, storm and structural failure, and they perished amidst the bursting shells of the flak batteries and the withering fire from the tenacious German night fighter defenders.

Ian Redmond

Chapter 1

Crewing Up

They stood in the makeshift hall at Wyton airfield, a rectangular brick building with a massive stone fireplace dominating one end of the room. One hundred complete strangers, fifty pilots and fifty navigators from various countries, had now been brought together in Cambridgeshire, England, to begin their tour of duty as Bomber Command crew members. The door opened and in strode Wing Commander G H (Geoff) Womersley, an Englishman who had been appointed the Station Commander for RAF Wyton in early 1944. At 29, he was older than most of men he would be commanding, but his experience as a bomber pilot, having flown 50 missions before being appointed to lead the 139 Squadron and earning a Distinguished Flying Cross in the process, meant that he fully understood the challenges facing his aircrews and the capabilities of the Mosquito aircraft that these new crews would be flying.

Wing Commander G H (Geoff) Womersley

"Gentleman," he began, "I will be returning in one hour and expect to have 50 aircrews in place," before turning smartly and exiting the room. Initial confusion over exactly how the assembled personnel were to pair themselves up was quickly overtaken by some good-natured attempts at advancing the process. One wiry fellow jumped onto a stool and shouted "Who wants a drunken navigator?"

"Not I," thought Flight Lieutenant Colin Bell, a 23-year-old Royal Air Force Mosquito bomber pilot, as he surveyed the room. A somewhat diminutive 5'6" tall and 154 pounds, Bell was an experienced pilot with over 1,000 hours of flight time to his credit, gained during his stint as a trainee with the United States Army Air Force. When the Japanese attacked Pearl Harbor, his role changed to that of a trainer of pilots, which added significantly more hours to his ledger.

As individuals began pairing up, Colin spied a large, serious looking man sitting by himself at the side of the room, wearing insignia that identified him as navigator and as a Canadian. Bell approached the man.

"Have you got yourself a pilot yet?"

"No," came the terse reply.

"What are your qualifications?" Bell inquired.

"I was senior navigation instructor at the Air Observer School in Chatham, New Brunswick, before becoming the Station Navigation Officer," came the response.

Bell was elated to have found someone who, like himself, had been an instructor prior to joining up. Without having had a lengthy conversation about interests, background, or why he was in the air force, Bell had already decided that the man seated before him was exactly the type of individual he wanted to fly with over Germany. If the Royal Canadian Air Force thought well enough of the man to have him instruct others in the art of navigation, then who was he to argue against his qualifications.

"You have a pilot now!"

Flight Lieutenant Douglas Redmond nodded, glad to have gotten through what he thought was an inefficient and somewhat foolish process and pleased to have paired up with someone who was highly qualified to fly the airplane that they would put their faith in. Redmond was a big man, 6'2" tall, with a strong physique developed through his time working in the forest as a lumberjack and his tenure as a fireman in western Canada. The 26-year-old navigator was a perfectionist when it came to his work, a serious, calm man whose sole focus was ensuring that he did his job to the best of his abilities, expecting nothing less from those around him. Not surprisingly, he put great value in the detail required to do any job right, and was pleased to find out that the smaller man with the big smile and the Errol Flynn moustache who stood before him had also been considered as a capable trainer of other pilots. With a wry smile, he looked at his new partner and said, "A bit like a marriage isn't it … 'til death do us part."

Bell sat down with his newfound comrade to await the return of the commanding officer. A few minutes later, WC Womersley reappeared, and seeing that the process had the desired results, approached each of the newly formed crews to gently suggest that it would be in their best interests to consider signing up for <u>two</u> tours of duty from the start of their service, promising that doing so would lead to "more interesting jobs." When he approached Colin and Doug with his offer, Bell pondered precisely what would constitute a more interesting job for a bomber crew, but remained quiet. Redmond, on the other hand, was quite clear about where he stood on the matter.

"I want a Victory Medal, not a Victoria Cross," he stated without hesitation.

Womersley, taken somewhat aback, looked to Bell for support. Bell, however, was of like mind, responding "Well, you have heard my navigator." A strong bond had already begun to form.

Colin Bell

Colin Bell had been born in Surrey, England, in 1921. At the outbreak of the war, he was living with his parents while studying to become a Chartered Surveyor. By 1939, his head filled with the exploits of the fictional squadron leader Biggles, Colin yearned to be a fighter pilot living in a world of machine guns and parachutes. In early 1940, he volunteered and soon after was called before a Selection Board at Oxford, where he was subjected to medical and fitness tests, math exams and, most daunting of all, an interview. He was asked by the admissions review panel why he wanted to fly. "I have a great interest in speed," he told them.

F/L Colin Bell

"What experience do you have with speed?"

"I drive a motorcycle," he replied.

Intrigued, a panel member asked what type he drove; his response of a two-stroke engine that Biggles would not have been caught dead on left the panel unimpressed, evidenced by the contemptuous laughter. All was not lost, however, as he also had an understanding of internal combustion engines. The panel explored the extent of his knowledge, asking him what the ratio was between the crank shaft and the drive shaft. "About half," Colin replied, secretly hoping that he had remembered that correctly. His response was well received, and after a short deliberation, Colin was informed that he was in and given the requisite piece of paper to prove it.

Colin was posted to the United States. Soon thereafter, he found himself stationed in Georgia where he successfully completed his pilot training and received his wings. His return to England was delayed when the Japanese attacked Pearl Harbor. Not long after the attack, he was summoned before the commanding officer, who immediately asked Colin, "I suppose you think you're going home?" As he had been training under the auspices of the United States Army Air Force, he was informed that he was now an advanced single engine flying instructor, responsible for training six American and British cadets.

"A bit like the blind leading the blind," he joked, which fell on deaf ears.

He finally returned to the United Kingdom in 1943, intending to pursue a career as a night fighter pilot. Upon hearing that the No. 8 Group were looking for pilots with over 1,000 hours of flying time to convert to Mosquito bombers, he applied for a transfer to RAF Bomber Command, which eventually brought him to Wyton.

Douglas Redmond

Doug Redmond was a Canadian born in Dean, a small community in the Musquodoboit Valley in Nova Scotia, in 1918. In his adolescent years, he gained considerable experience in the local lumber industry, attaining the position of foreman by the age of sixteen. While adept with an axe and saw, it was his skills in mathematics and science that led him to becoming an expert lumber grader. In early 1940, he attempted to enlist in the Royal Canadian Air Force for aircrew training but was denied because at that time they were only accepting university graduates. Soon thereafter, he made his way to British Columbia, in western Canada, where he was hired as a fireman by the City of Trail. All the while, Doug kept in contact with the RCAF recruiting office. Perhaps in response to his persistence, the recruiting office hinted that if he went to their district office in Calgary, Alberta, he might be accepted. Without hesitation, he made the trip and was accepted in August of 1941.

F/L Douglas Redmond

In November of that year, Doug was posted to Lethbridge, Alberta, to the No. 8 Bombing and Gunnery School. Due to his high marks, he was paraded before the Squadron Leader who informed him that he was being sent to Observer School. He subsequently graduated from there at the top of the class and not long after became the senior instructor. In 1943, he was posted to Chatham, New Brunswick, to improve on his navigation skills and to train staff pilots in navigation. Finally, in July 1944, he made his way to England, where he took additional training before making his way to RAF Wyton.

Rapid Introductions

The selection process now complete, the two men spent the next week getting acquainted. Over the course of seven days, the newly formed crew flew eight times to familiarize themselves with each other and the airplane. During these flights, it was common to fly the Mosquito at heights barely above the tree tops. After the initial low-level flight, Doug looked at Colin and grumbled, "I didn't need to join the air force to be killed by a tree. I could have done that at home working in the forest."

During these flights, the friendship grew as they discussed many topics.

"Colin, how did you come to be a pilot?"

"Well, I can remember when I was a young lad," Colin replied, "my father would take me to the Hendon Aerodrome to see the Royal Air Force Display Show. In those days, the show was typically made up of biplanes that would make mock bombing runs on a native village, after which the troops would rush in and win the battle."

"It was pretty heady stuff for a young boy, the stuff of dreams," he said, gazing out at the countryside as it raced by the cockpit window. He paused and a look of sadness crossed his face. "But in 1940, bitter reality replaced romantic fiction. On my way to visit my girlfriend, a stray German aircraft flew overhead and lobbed a bomb out, landing on a home on the opposite side of the road from where I was walking. After a violent crash, I and everything around me was covered in a cloud of dust and debris. The house was gone, as I would have been too if it had been a bigger bomb. It was at that moment I realized that this could not be allowed to continue, so I set my mind on joining the RAF."

Doug too felt the need to sign up and enter the battle. The German war machine had reached into Atlantic Canada. It was widely known that German submarines had penetrated Halifax harbour, even landing men in Labrador to establish weather stations on the coast. While Canada was far removed from the battlefield, the local population in Halifax was well aware of the potential for enemy espionage. In response, the City instituted rules about where one could walk. If you were caught on the wrong side of the street, you were considered as a possible German spy.

For Doug, his heart and mind were with the British Empire. "My family came from Ireland in the 1800s and the Canadian ties to Europe are still strong. I couldn't sit idly by and watch country after country be ground under the boot of an evil puppet master." Deep down, he believed that if the Germans went unchecked, they would eventually turn their eyes to North America, with Hitler bent on world domination.

Through the course of discussions, jammed into the cramped confines of their Mosquito, the two men soon learned that they shared a common story in their youth. In 1927, while attending his lessons in the one-room school house near his home in rural Nova Scotia, Doug recalled the day the teacher led them outside for a break in their lessons. "As we stood outside the school, a single engine plane passed overhead. The teacher told us that the plane we had seen was on its way to Paris on a solo transatlantic flight," Doug explained. While none of the students had any idea who Charles Lindbergh was, the idea of flying sparked Doug's imagination.

"Extraordinary, Doug! I had a similar experience", recounted Colin. "My father took me to Croydon Aerodrome, where we climbed up on the roof of one of the buildings and watched Lindbergh fly in after leaving Paris at the completion of his Atlantic crossing!"

Chapter 2

608 Squadron, Royal Air Force

The newly formed duo was assigned to the 608 Squadron flying out of RAF Downham Market, located in the west of the County of Norfolk in England. The squadron was a member of Bomber Command's No. 8 Group's Light Night Striking Force, with the Mosquitoes filling the role of Pathfinders.

Pathfinder squadrons were established by the RAF to spearhead raids, acting as target finders for the main body of bombers that would follow behind them. The concept was simple. The Pathfinders were made up of the best and most experienced operational crews that were available within Bomber Command. They would lead the night attack, arriving ahead of the heavy bombers and marking the target with flares so as to improve the accuracy of the subsequent

Pathfinder crew pin (Source: Author's collection)

bombing. The Pathfinders were led by a Master Bomber who would release the initial target indicator. He was supported by a second-in-command flying in a following aircraft in case he was shot down or failed to mark the target accurately. The rest of the Pathfinder crews would release their target indicator flares in turn over top of the lead bomber's markers to identify the precise target buildings for the following main force of bombers. This practice was not without risk, as evidenced by the fact that during the three years over which the Pathfinders flew, they suffered dreadfully, losing a staggering 3,727 men during the course of operations.

With a motto of *Omnibus ungulis* ("*with all talons*"), 608 Squadron prided itself on its ability to attack quickly and effectively, a strategy made possible by the Mosquito bombers that made up the squadron's arsenal.

From its inception in August of 1944, 608 Squadron engaged in strategic bombing of industrial areas throughout Germany, including the cities of Bremen, Magdeburg, Dresden, Hamburg, Nuremburg and Berlin. Flying predominantly at night, the squadron carried out 1,774 attacks until the end of the war, 1,711 of which were

608 Squadron Insignia
(Source: Author's collection)

successfully carried out against primary targets, with only 17 being diverted to secondary targets. The squadron's actions were not without cost, as the squadron lost 21 Mosquitoes and 18 air crews over ten months of service, with a further two crew members killed in a flying accident in June 1945.

With the arrival of the new flight crews, RAF Downham Market was now home to some 2,500 men and women. The base was alive with aircrew, groundcrew, administrators, medical staff, security details, meteorologists, motor pool mechanics, communications and intelligence personnel, and others, all focussed on doing their part to support the tasks assigned to the squadron. Given the desire to have these squadrons manned by the best personnel available, Pathfinder aircrews were comprised of a unique mixture of nationalities among the pilots and navigators. This was certainly the case for 608 Squadron as over the course of the squadron's brief operational life, RAF Downham Market

608 Squadron aircrews, September 1944
(Colin Bell, seated, front row, left; Doug Redmond, standing, row 2, far left)

was home to crewmen from virtually every Allied nation. During their six months of flying with the squadron, Colin and Doug would share the highs and lows of life in the RAF with a collection of Dutch, Czech, Norwegian, Canadian, Australian, New Zealander, Irish, English, Scot, and Welsh airmen and groundcrew.

All of these men had significant experience; pilots tended to have at least 1,000 hours of flying time under their belt, whereas navigators, in addition to having logged significant hours of flight time, were those who had demonstrated the highest degree of skill in mastering the various methods of navigation. Indeed, there were many in the squadron who were on their second, and sometimes third, tours of duty, having chosen to remain active because of the lure of flying in the Mosquito.

Chapter 3

RAF Downham Market

The airfield at RAF Downham Market was a sprawling site with its supporting infrastructure and associated buildings spread over several acres. For newly arrived aircrew, it was easy to get lost, so the first bit of business for newcomers was to get oriented with their new home.

Upon arrival, Colin and Doug found their assigned housing and then met up again to explore their surroundings. It did not take long to realize that the distance between the dormitories and the airfield and its working buildings was considerable. The base housing was situated south of the main runway, with the five dormitory sites scattered around the site's flat terrain. Consisting of corrugated metal half-moons bolted onto concrete slabs, the accommodations, known formally as Nissen huts or less formally as Iron Lungs, were spartan at best, with each hut holding between eight and eighteen people. "I can't say I am too fussy about the quarters," said Doug as they checked out their new home. While both men spoke English, each had a distinctive accent. At first it required that they pay close attention to what the other was saying to be sure that messages were fully understood. For Colin, the challenge was to adapt to Doug's

Atlantic Canadian accent, variations of which could be found across Canada's Maritime provinces. As they spoke about their training or how they came to Downham Market, Doug would insert the occasional 'r' in the middle of a word. "Have you seen the warshing up area yet?" This was counterbalanced by the removal of a letter where it was deemed as superfluous. "I noticed that there were a few men at the train station that were part of the 'reglar' army."

Over time, Colin also learned that if Doug did not know a person's name, they immediately became known as Buddy. At the outset of their time at Downham Market, most everyone working at the station was greeted by Doug as Buddy. Even more astounding to Colin was Doug's total disdain for swearing. "Bah, it is just a sign of a lack of education. One can always find the right words to express one's feelings."

For Doug, he had to quickly attune himself to Colin's educated British accent, complete with the RAF slang. It was not uncommon for Doug to look quizzically at his compatriot when he made references to things like "bumfodder" (toilet paper) or "penguins" (groundcrew who did not fly). He also had to stay sharp because Colin was armed with a devil-may-care attitude and was quick to make a joke.

The pair made their way south of the huts, walking towards a mixture of brick and stone structures. They quickly discovered the old St. Mary's vicarage, known as Bexwell, which served as the Officers Mess, and several more huts. "That looks like a canteen," said Colin as they explored the various buildings, "and that appears to be the post office." Nearby, the two men found the camp stores. Upon closer inspection, they saw that the final pair of buildings housed a gymnasium and some sort of training facility.

"This is like the village square," said Doug as they continued past the Rectory and the base chapel.

"Just missing a pub and a fish and chips shop," responded Colin.

After further wandering, the two men learned that the dormitory for the Women's Auxiliary Air Force was in a separate location, complete with its own Mess and associated camp facilities. "Seems like a wise move," said Doug.

"I suspect that even with this separation there will be considerable distraction!" chimed in Colin with a smile.

As they made their way back to their respective huts, they spied a small building that was isolated from the rest of the camp.

"Hey Buddy," Doug said to a passerby, "what is that building over there?"

"That's the camp hospital," came the response.

"Good to know," replied Colin with some bravado. "For others that is, as we shan't be needing it."

Having mentally mapped the layout of their new home, Colin pointed out that there seemed to be an unusually large number of bicycles on the base. The rationale for the bikes soon became clear. Ground staff who lived in the Nissen huts had to cover a significant distance in order to reach their work areas near the airfield on time. They soon learned that bicycles were also the preferred means of travelling to the nearby town of Downham Market, two miles northeast of the airfield.

As they strode back to the camp, they looked out over the actual airfield in the distance. The airfield itself was comprised of three runways, two of 1,400 yards and one at

RAF Downham Market, 1944

2,000 yards, each of which was 150 feet wide. The three runways were linked by three miles of sixty-foot-wide perimeter tracks. This part of the base had been a major construction project prior to the base opening in 1942, and required enough concrete to build eleven miles of modern three lane highway.

Lining the main runway was a pipeline that supported an innovative system designed to improve the airfield's ability to operate in any weather. The system, known as either "Fog Investigation and Dispersal Operations" or "Fog, Intensive, Disposal Of", was referred to colloquially as FIDO.

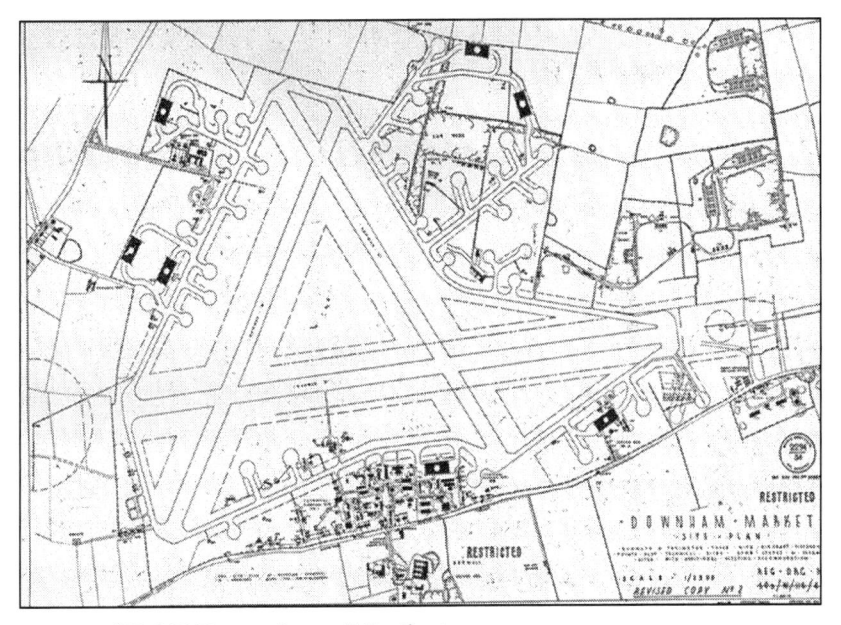

Map of RAF Downham Market
(Source: 218 Squadron.wordpress.com)

FIDO facilitated the landing of aircraft in low visibility by burning enormous amounts of petrol which was pumped through large diameter pipes from a storage tank at the edge of the airfield. The flames would provide sufficient heat to burn off the low-lying fog. The supply pipes were placed in concrete troughs running alongside the runway in recognition of the possibility of an inadvertent accident or crash of an aircraft. The pipes were also fitted with isolating valves that allowed the flow of fuel to be shut down to any section that might be damaged.

Circling the field were the facilities for aircraft maintenance and the airfield administration area. Four hangars supported the squadron, two to the northeast of the runways and two to the northwest. The station and dispersal buildings were located to the south of the main runway and consisted of a mixture of Nissen huts and small brick buildings. Nestled in the midst of these buildings was the station's control tower, the most prominent fixture on the base, and the crew locker rooms.

Colin and Doug quickly acclimatized to their new surroundings. Having arrived in early fall, they were relieved to have missed what was described to them as living quarters that were unbearably hot. Within a few months, however, they would yearn for warmer temperatures, as the Nissen huts were frigidly cold in the winter months owing to their metal and concrete design. Each hut came with a small coal burning stove expressly intended to heat the interior.

Unfortunately, the weekly allotment of only one bucket of coal meant that the available fuel supply did not allow for the adequate warming of the living quarters.

As the weeks passed, the two men learned various heating tricks from their colleagues. It was not uncommon to see men sliding reading lamps between the sheets with the light on while heading out for a drink, hoping to return from the pub to a warm bed. More conventional approaches used the small stoves as much as possible by supplementing the small amount of coal with other combustible materials. Colin and Doug discovered that, for those living in the huts, a considerable amount of time was spent scrounging additional material to burn for heat, the most popular source being the trees that lined the periphery of the airfield. So cold was the winter of 1944, however, that the base and surrounding area suffered a wood shortage; the shortage was so acute that the winter was marked by the disappearance of fence posts and signage around the base.

As winter progressed, it was not uncommon for many to dress in layers, particularly when retiring for the evening. Even the camp's contingent of Canadians, many of whom had experienced harsher winters than their squadron mates, complained about the "goddamned climate."

The cold wasn't the only issue for those living on the base. The area's low-lying topography, punctuated by nearby wetlands known as fens, meant that the camp was prone to dampness. When the camp was first constructed in 1943, the Station Medical Officer sought to condemn the huts due their excessive dampness and the resulting respiratory issues that developed amongst base personnel. Those living in the Iron Lungs soon learned that the limited heat put out by the small stoves did not keep out the damp; in fact, the metal shell of the huts attracted condensation. Whenever someone left clothes by the stove to dry, the huts had a tendency to fill with steam, only adding to the pervading dampness.

Life at the airfield was punctuated by constant activity, both in the air and on the ground. On days where operations were scheduled, aircrews would be preparing to fly that night, spending the day in briefings, poring over intelligence reports on recent actions, test flying to ensure aircraft readiness for the evening's action or finding distractions to take their minds off the coming sortie. Ground crews spent their time servicing the squadron's aircraft, ensuring that each was ready for the evening's mission. Others spent the day developing briefings and gathering additional meteorological data to supplement the information provided by RAF Headquarters.

Colin and Doug quickly adopted the daily patterns that made up life on an air base. They rose early each morning to face the unpleasant task of washing and shaving at the communal basin with what was often cold water. "Of course, it is cold. Everything here is cold. Bloody climate," grumbled Doug as he towelled off and joined Colin prior to making their way to the Mess for breakfast. Bacon and eggs, often real eggs, were the basic staple, supplemented with bread. There was, in fact, so much bread available that crew members would often take it back to their quarters to be toasted on the stove later in the day.

If there were no missions scheduled, and any required duties were completed, Colin and Doug would entertain themselves as best they could. It was not uncommon for Doug to engage in games that kept his mind sharp, such as bridge, chess, or checkers. On rare occasions, he might even join a spirited game of small-stakes poker with the Australians or the South Africans. "Never play for more than you can comfortably lose" was his mantra. Having lived in rural Canada during the Great Depression, Doug had grown up doing farm chores early in the morning and late in the day, hunting and fishing for the family's sustenance, and biking into the woods to work at the lumber mill. Survival was a struggle and the limited amount of money was not to be frittered away frivolously. With that in mind, the amount that he was prepared to wager was very small.

For Colin, the daily routine changed within weeks of his arriving at RAF Downham Market with the arrival of his bride, who moved into the nearby village. Colin and Kath had married in 1943 and had had little opportunity to be together since that time. The small apartment that she took soon became Colin's home away from the air base and the destination of choice whenever he could be there. Although

Kath was living in close proximity to her husband, it did little to reduce her apprehension associated with the uncertainty of bomber crews flying in harm's way. Knowing that Colin was flying on a given night meant little sleep while awaiting his return. If the plane did not return as anticipated, as would happen on more than one occasion, the resulting increase in anxiety was hard to bear.

Doug too had married in 1943, but his wife Hazel was several thousand miles away in rural Nova Scotia. Relying solely on regular letters, Doug and Hazel were able to keep in contact. However, unlike Kath, who would see Colin on a frequent basis, Hazel did not know when the air crew was flying, where they were going, or when they would return. In many senses, life on the home front was even more stressful for Hazel because the uncertainty was her constant companion. As far as she knew, Doug could be in the air every day. In order to cope with the stress, Hazel frequently made the trip to Halifax to visit the harbour and watch the navy vessels coming and going. Often times, she would see soldiers, many of whom were wounded, disembarking, their tours of duty over. Though bittersweet, she did take some comfort in the knowledge that men did come home from war.

As the two men adjusted to their new lives, in November 1944, a new man arrived to lead the squadron, Wing Commander Robert Clifford (Cliff) Alabaster; an Englishman who had begun his RAF career as an air observer on twin-engine Whitley bombers before receiving training as navigator and subsequently assuming that role on a Lancaster. A highly skilled man, he had the unusual distinction of being appointed captain of his aircraft even though he was the navigator. By the time he arrived at RAF Downham Market, he had already flown over 80 sorties, a number that would grow to 100 during his tenure with the 608 Squadron.

Alabaster, recognizing the importance of strong morale, quickly established what became know as the Welfare Fund. Each month, all base personnel (aircrew and groundcrew) contributed one day's wages to the fund. The fund was then used to purchase amenities designed to improve the lives of those assigned to the squadron. While proceeds from the fund were used to acquire books for a small library and pay for the installation of a big, open fireplace in the Crew Room, the predominant function of the resources was to facilitate the large parties that took place on a fairly regular basis.

WC Cliff Alabaster

On the appointed day, the festivities would often begin with a football (soccer) match pitting aircrew against groundcrew. For Canadians like Doug, soccer was not a familiar game, so the contest was a bit of a mismatch, although the participants quite willingly gave it their all. At the end of the hotly contested game, usually won by the groundcrew, participants would clean up, board a five-ton truck, and head into the neighbouring village for an evening of excessive drinking and merry making.

For the English members of the base, such behaviour harkened back to the times of the ancient Britons, whose practice it was to allow their armies to release their energy in a similar manner between battles. Over time, these sojourns became known as visits from "Alabaster's Forty Thieves", often highlighted by the Wing Commander leading the singing of the popular music of the day, interspersed with the occasional bawdy song.

Morale was also addressed through other means, including movies that were shown in the Sergeant's Mess, card games, and an infrequent dance. Social activities were not, however, limited solely to those on the base. The town and the other neighbouring villages also offered pleasant distractions from the daily activities of a military installation actively involved in the war. Just two miles from the RAF station, the town of Downham Market offered several venues to reduce the anxieties and tensions associated with the war.

For those who sought distraction through motion pictures, one had the opportunity to go to the movies at the Regent Cinema in the heart of town. Recognizing that showing the same film over and over was not good business, the Regent made it a practice to have a variety of films available, usually changing its program twice a week, with two shows scheduled on Saturday to accommodate more people. If movies were not of interest, the town also offered dances twice a week at the Town Hall, where base personnel and the local population could mingle and, not surprisingly, explore short- or long-term relationships.

For the population of the Town of Downham Market, having an RAF airfield as its immediate neighbour significantly altered their pre-war way of life. Gone was the idyllic country setting with its quiet lanes and countryside. In its place was a bustling, noisy military installation that was a beehive of activity at all hours. Residents soon learned that the novelty of having an airfield nearby was replaced by the incessant, high level of noise and the greatly increased amount of road traffic in and out of the facility, all of which now clogged the local roads. On top of that, there was the ever-present possibility of German air raids targeting the airfield that might inadvertently (or perhaps deliberately) result in bombs dropping within the town. The quiet rural lifestyle that existed pre-war had quickly vanished with the construction of the RAF base.

Local residents came to know that the impacts of the air base could be both direct and personal. It was not uncommon for the RAF to evict landowners from their property in order that it be put to use for military purposes, or to ban the use of lands for previously enjoyed activities

such as hunting or fishing. If the physical impacts were not jarring enough, the influx of base personnel looking to either release pent up tension or seek distraction from the monotony of daily duty brought with it the need to reconsider traditional standards, morals, and values. Despite the changes to their lives and lifestyles, many of the local families opened their homes to the airmen, offering a chance to share a fire and some pleasant conversation over coffee. Base personnel greatly appreciated the warmth, comfort, and camaraderie, preferring it to the small stoves in the ever-cold Nissen huts. In return for their kindness, the guests from the base
often repaid the townsfolk by taking on odd jobs or assisting with harvesting.

When not in the air, Colin and Doug frequently made the two-mile trek into town. Before long, the pair had found a number of places that provided the sought-after distractions from the anxiety-laden lives they led as Bomber Command crew. It was not uncommon for the two men to be seen walking or cycling through the market town's rusty-ginger coloured sandstone and pale-yellow brick buildings as they made their way to the centre of town. It was here that the main streets came together under a quaint, 19th century cast-iron clock tower to form the Market Square, the destination of choice for all manner of things.

If it was cigarettes that you sought, then one would pay a visit to Stannard's shop, which, as an added bonus, also served cups of tea and cakes or light meals that provided a welcome change from the camp fare. Those seeking a more substantive meal had several options, including Sly's Café on

*The market square in the Town of Downham Market
(Source: Andy Moore)*

High Street, a particularly popular venue with air crew, as those who returned late from raids, and having missed breakfast in the Mess, could find a decent morning meal at a reasonable price. The Temperance Hotel also offered a breakfast of ham and eggs for those that were so inclined, while the Castle Hotel was the favoured spot for the higher ranked personnel, due in large part to its more fashionable décor and its practice of providing accommodation for airmen's wives when they visited during stand-down periods.

Perhaps the biggest draws were the various pubs and clubs found in the area. Colin and Doug often found their way to the Crown Hotel for a few pints of beer and the offer of food at closing time. Other village pubs provided the ideal atmosphere for a few drinks and conversation with friends, the perfect tonic for reducing the stress of facing possible death on a regular basis. So popular were the various watering holes that Station Police were often employed to summon aircrews back to base to prepare for their next operation.

It was not uncommon for 608 Squadron personnel to be found in the same bar with members of the 635 Squadron, the Lancaster crews with whom they shared RAF Downham Market. While the two groups seldom interacted, 608 Squadron personnel did enjoy giving their colleagues grief about the nature of their operations. The Lancasters' operations were frequently focussed in the Pas de Calais region of France, while the 608's actions were deeper into Germany. When the 635 crews lamented the time they spent over targets, the derisive comments would soon follow.

"How long were you over enemy territory? Ten minutes … God, how awful!" was a common refrain, usually followed by some colourful language. The final word, in most cases, fell to the Mosquito aircrews, who taunted their fellow airmen with chants of "Get east of the Rhine."

For others, alcohol and food were not what drew them to the town. Many personnel frequented the 13th century church located on the hill near the Market Square to seek comfort and strength, or strolled along the river to decompress after a stressful mission. On occasions where lucky personnel had a few days of leave, Downham Market was the connecting point for trains to London and the excitement and diversion that the great city could offer.

Ian Redmond

Chapter 4

The de Havilland Mosquito

In 1939, the Air Ministry's focus was on developing large, armed aircraft. At that time, the first proposal for a two-engine wooden bomber that carried no armament was given only a lukewarm reception. Undaunted by the initial limited interest, the de Havilland Aircraft Company continued to pursue its proposal, pitching the Mosquito design at every

The de Havilland Mosquito

opportunity. The designers had a number of compelling arguments to put forward in support of their aircraft, most significant of which was that the all wooden construction significantly reduced the weight of the aircraft which, when combined with the use of two Rolls Royce Merlin engines, produced unparalleled speed.

The de Havilland team also armed themselves with strong tactical arguments in support of the production of the Mosquito. Firstly, Mosquitoes were made of plywood – a balsa core between two thin layers of yellow birch veneer. As such, the Company argued that the construction of a wooden plane would not draw vital metals away from other war production needs. Secondly, building the Mosquito would not require taking workers away from metal-based projects. Thirdly, de Havilland contended that Mosquito production could utilize unskilled labourers who would easily become experts in wood utilization without the need for technical training. Finally, they pointed out that a wooden bomber would be far easier and faster to repair should it be damaged during operations.

After considering the merits of the proposal, the Air Ministry agreed to the construction of a prototype, with the proviso that production was not to interfere with the production of Tiger Moths and Oxford trainers that were currently on the assembly line. Work began in earnest on the development of the first prototype, with the first test flight occurring on November 25, 1940. The prototype was a sleek, silver-toned machine with the soon-to-be easily recognized tapered fuselage, twin engines and three-bladed propellers. The initial 30-minute flight was successful, with the plane easily cruising at 220 miles per hour.

By May of 1941, the Mosquito was being clocked at speeds of 392 mph. That following October, the first Mosquitoes were delivered. As the Air Ministry still believed that any true bomber had to be equipped with guns of some sort to protect itself, the first Mosquitoes were not considered bombers. The next iteration of the aircraft rolled off the line in June 1942, complete with four-blade propellers, special exhaust flame dampers and the capacity to carry a load of 500-pound bombs. By October, design changes had enabled high-altitude flying through the use of pressurized cabins but, more importantly, the aircraft was now flying 421 to 424 mph at high altitudes. Given that the fastest American fighters in operation at that time, the P-51 Mustang and the P-47 Thunderbolt, had maximum speeds of 430 and 416 mph respectively at heights of 22,000 to 25,000 feet, the new Mosquito was now the one of the fastest operational aircraft at high altitudes in existence. More importantly, the plane was faster than anything the German Air Force could put in the air against it at that time, including the principal night fighter employed by the Luftwaffe, the Focke Wulf 190 (FW 190), which flew at 408 mph at 20,600 feet. (Price, 1969).

By 1943, Bomber Command's arsenal of aircraft relied extensively on the heavily armed four-engine bomber which now dominated the night skies over Europe. While able to carry huge payloads over great distances, the heavy bombers were lumbering aircraft in comparison to the German fighters that rose to meet them in combat. The introduction of the Mosquito to the RAF's arsenal during this time period would have significant impacts on the execution of the strategic bombing offensive moving forward. The appearance of an aircraft capable of lightning strikes against targets deep in Germany was a welcome addition.

With its 2,000-pound payload capacity and a range of over 1,900 miles with auxiliary fuel tanks, a Mosquito could deliver significant striking power at a higher speed than the conventional heavy bomber. As an illustration, a Mosquito could strike at Berlin and return to base within an average of 4.5 hours. A Lancaster attacking the same target could expect to be in the air for over eight hours. While the heavy bombers could carry more ordinance, their relatively slow airspeed made them more susceptible to German air defences. By the end of the war, the "wooden wonder" was able to carry a bomb load to Berlin that matched that of the Flying Fortress and other four-engine aircraft that required crews of almost a dozen men.

As previously noted, one of the most significant benefits of the Mosquito was its speed. The light-weight frame, powered by two Merlin engines, provided the bomber with significantly more air speed than any of the propeller driven German fighters that were operational at that time, making the prey more elusive to the hunters. Mosquitos travelled so high and so fast that very few enemy fighters at the same altitude could catch them. Even with their advantages, the Mosquito aircrew could never be so arrogant as to assume that they were invincible to attacks by German aircraft. It was, in fact, commonly understood that for every Mosquito flying over Berlin there was an FW 190 circling, eager to get a shot at taking it down. A formidable fighter in its own right, the FW 190 provided greater firepower than the Messerschmitt Bf 109 and, at low to medium altitude, superior manoeuvrability. Even though it is often cited as one of the best fighter planes of World War II, possessing a maximum speed of around 400 mph at 20,000 feet, it was unable to match the speed of the Mosquito bomber at higher altitudes. In response, the Luftwaffe developed the practice of stacking FW 190s over targeted cities at 30,000 feet or more to give them a height and diving speed advantage. Wild Boar squadrons, as the Luftwaffe referred to them, would only have one chance to dive down on unsuspecting bombers. If they missed on their first dive, it was generally too late to mount a second attack. For the Mosquito crew, the key to survival was being ever vigilant, constantly scanning the skies for signs of circling fighters. If they were seen, an equivalent dive by the bomber would ensure that they sped away unharmed.

As part of a morale boosting exercise, one deskbound Air Ministry official produced a poster showing a nonchalant pilot holding a beer and saying "Who's afraid of the Focke

Wulf 190". When displayed in 608's Flight Hut, one of the squadron commanders wrote underneath "We are" and signed his name. Everyone else in the squadron soon signed as well. Realism and common sense were more effective than propaganda when you were fighting to stay alive.

The Mosquito squadrons quickly developed a reputation for sudden strikes against tactical and strategic targets through such sorties as those against a German prison in Amiens, France, that allowed members of the French underground to escape, or the raid in Berlin that interrupted an on-air radio broadcast by Reichsmarschall Hermann Goering and, later that same day, a rally being led by Joseph Goebbels outside of Berlin. It did not take long for the Mosquito to gain the respect of the Germans.

In response to the threats posed by the wooden bomber, Hermann Goering established two special wings of enhanced fighters to deal with the Mosquito menace, both of which were disbanded in 1943 having failed to down a single bomber. In fact, the Luftwaffe so respected and hated the Mosquito that they instituted a rule that a German pilot who downed a Mosquito was credited with two kills.

Indeed, so impressed were the Germans that they began to design their own wooden aircraft, which they dubbed the "Moskito" in deference to the de Havilland success. The German prototype first flew in July 1943 and, although seemingly clumsy in appearance and somewhat bulkier than its RAF opponent, it flew at an impressive 435 mph during testing. (Holliday, 1970). Unlike the RAF aircraft, the Moskito was armed with two 20-mm cannons and two 30-mm cannons which, to the consternation of the German designers, caused considerable vibration of the entire aircraft when the cannons were fired. In the end, however, the lack of skilled labour required to build the plane, and the designer's belief that the use of wood did not lend itself to a smooth finish, caused the project to be dropped.

For the crews that manned the Mosquito, it quickly cemented its reputation as the best aircraft in the world and affectionately earned the nickname "Mossie". The versatile aircraft excelled at its ability to perform as a fighter, an unarmed bomber, a reconnaissance aircraft, a high-speed transport plane, a pathfinder, a carrier-based torpedo plane or a spoof raider, and fulfilled all of these roles with a minimum casualty rate. Indeed, the Mosquito ended the war with the lowest loss rate of any aircraft in RAF Bomber Command service.

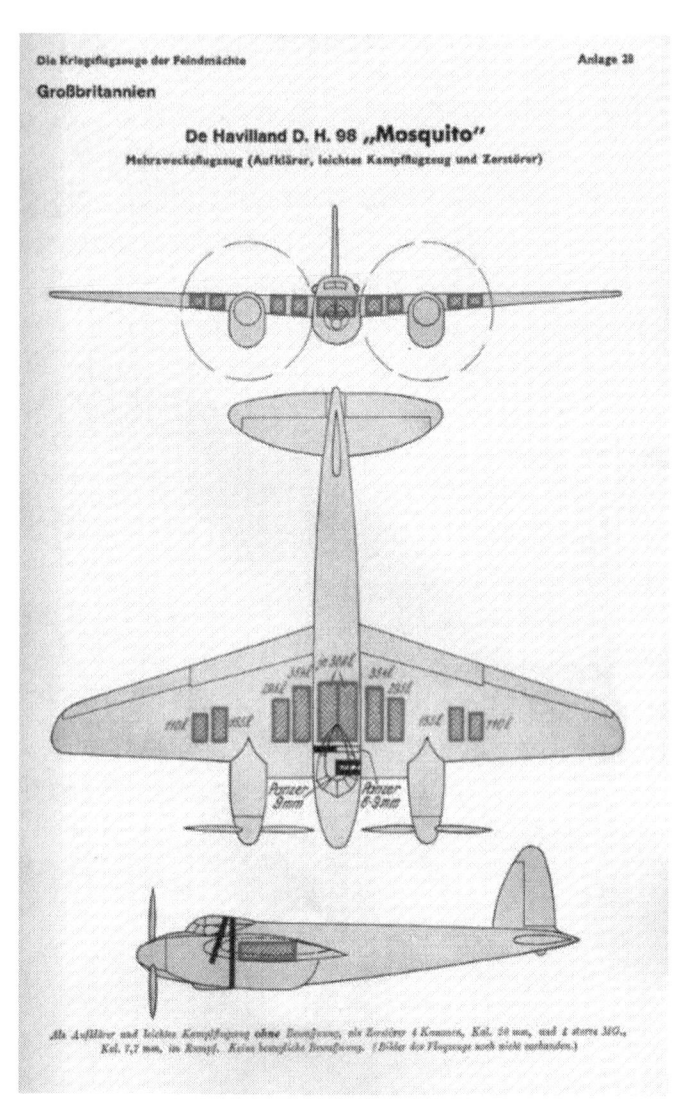

*Mosquito Identification for German Pilots
(Source: Lancasterbombers.net)*

Chapter 5

September 1944 – Into the Breach

By September of 1944, many believed that the war was moving to its conclusion, with an Allied victory by Christmas seen to be almost certain. The Russian army was approaching the eastern frontiers of Germany, while the British and American forces were advancing through Italy, and the Canadian, American, and British armies that had landed in Normandy in June were now closing on the Rhine, having liberated France from Nazi occupation.

The British 2nd Army, under General Bernard Montgomery, entered Brussels on September 3rd, following up the next day by taking Antwerp, with its docks intact. Three days later, Montgomery's men had forced their way across the Albert Canal. Meanwhile, the U.S. 1st Army supporting Montgomery on the right, had taken Namur on the day of the capture of Antwerp and was nearing Aachen. Farther to the south, General George Patton's U.S. 3rd Army, having raced forward to take Verdun on August 31, was already beginning to cross the Moselle River near Metz on September 5, heightening the possibility of achieving a breakthrough into Germany's economically important Saarland.

The Allies' amazing advance of 350 miles in a few weeks came to a crashing halt by the end of the month. Nonetheless, in early September the U.S. and British forces had had a combined superiority of 20 to 1 in tanks and 25 to 1 in aircraft over the Germans. The Germans, however, still held their industrial heartlands of the Ruhr Valley and the Saarland.

Hannover – September 5th

Training flights were over. Colin and Doug were now an operational crew in the 608 Squadron. While some might speak of being anxious to get into the show, and others might express fear of what might lie ahead, this particular Canuck and Brit team were outwardly calm. Colin would say that there was no time to consider what the future might hold, one just focussed on the task at hand. Doug calmly went about his business, exhibiting a consistently confident and cool demeanor, a trademark that would certainly come to serve him and Colin well in the coming months.

For now, they waited. With twenty-one aircrews now assigned to Downham Market, there was an odd competitive feel to being selected for any given mission because the squadron only had twelve operational aircraft available for use. Not surprisingly, some crews expressed frustration with the selection process and the amount of down time between sorties. For Colin and Doug, the inevitability of the first sortie dominated their thoughts with an equal mix of excitement and trepidation.

Early in the morning of September 5, 1944, RAF High Wycombe, Bomber Command's headquarters, was already a beehive of activity. The daily target determination conference was well underway. Senior commanders listened as meteorologists and intelligence officers presented current information on the projected weather forecasts for western Europe, details of potential objectives for attack, and an indication of the available aircraft. After a short period of deliberation, the Commander-in-Chief chose the targets.

Operations staff immediately began the detailed planning and alerted each of the Bomber Groups. Once informed, each Group Headquarters decided which of its squadrons would participate in the raids. At ten a.m., the details on the proposed raid were transmitted to 608 Squadron via the red scrambler telephone in the airfield's operation room, after which the information was transcribed onto the squadron's operations board. The squadron's planners reviewed the details on the operation and determined which planes and aircrews would participate. This data was then provided to the station commander, squadron commanders, and the squadron's intelligence officer. Shortly thereafter, the word went out that the squadron was going to be operating that evening, with details to be revealed at a noon hour briefing.

A steady increase of activity followed as the squadron began its preparations. Selected crews were notified, planes identified, and all related information was transmitted back to Group Command. Once done, attention turned to the determination of navigation routes, departure times, and fuel and bomb loads. Maps and briefing materials were also prepared for use with the selected air crews. The base's meteorological officer would supplement the morning's data by monitoring air pressure, wind speed, and weather conditions through the use of weather balloons. Once all of the essential facts and figures were compiled, the briefings were finalized.

At the same time, the groundcrews pored over the aircraft to prepare them for the evening flight. The crew of engine and airframe fitters undertook minor repairs and adjustments while taking on any additional last-minute jobs. Typically, the groundcrew did their work in the open which, given the blustery weather conditions common to late fall and winter, meant that the team spent many hours servicing aircraft while exposed to whatever Mother Nature could throw at them. Their single-minded focus was to get the plane ready as quickly as possible. The aircrews came to rely on their supporting team, recognizing that their work reduced the likelihood of the Mosquito malfunctioning during a mission. Colin and Doug would quickly come to appreciate the efforts of the groundcrew and, at the end of each successful flight, it would become part of their routine to give their rum ration to their supporting team to thank them.

As the day progressed, Colin and Doug did their best to relax but found it difficult knowing that they were about to go on their first mission. While both men were highly experienced in terms of their respective roles, having both put in significant time flying and having trained others in their areas of expertise, they had never been exposed to the life of active combat and the reality of flying over occupied Europe and into the heart of Germany, where the enemy focus was on knocking them out of the sky.

At 12:00 hours, the affected aircrews assembled in the Briefing Room near the Control Tower. At the appointed hour, Group Captain Wallace Kyle, the commanding officer for the base, arrived to lead the briefing. Surveying the assembled men, he began with a roll call of crew captains.

"Gentlemen, I know you are anxious to know where you are going this evening, so let's get to it." At this point, a curtain on the end wall was pulled back to reveal a large map of north-western Europe marked with the night's target. On this day, 608 Squadron was tasked with attacking Hannover, Germany.

Hannover, an important railway junction that connected two major east-west and north-south rail lines, was an active industrial centre in the Third Reich producing tires and other rubber parts for military vehicles and aircraft, guns and tracked-vehicles, batteries for submarines, and torpedoes. In addition, the northeastern outskirts of the city produced gasoline and motor oils for the Luftwaffe. As the briefing progressed, it was clear that the refineries were the focus for the evening's action.

The crews were provided with precise details on the routes to be taken to and from the target, including identification of turning points. This was followed by exact instructions for the target area that indicated what flares would be used in specific conditions, and the final details on the run in to the target. Crews were also provided with the colours of the day that would be used by crews to identify emergency situations, such as a wounded man on board a returning aircraft. Considerable data was provided on the weather, including cloud height, freezing levels, and icing indexes. This was followed by a report by the squadron intelligence officer (known by those on the base as "the Spy") on what could be expected in terms of enemy opposition during the raid, including the likelihood of night fighters over the target and the anticipated level of anti-aircraft fire. As a rookie crew, the pair just nodded. Being told that a moderate level of anti-aircraft fire was expected would only take on a full meaning later that day.

Once the briefing was completed, Doug sat down with his fellow navigators to discuss flight plans. As Mosquitoes had only a two-man crew, the navigator was also responsible for aiming and dropping the bombs. Once routes were known, the navigators then determined the bomb settings to be used. As each man copied down the raid's details, Doug pored over a large wall map of Europe with areas of German defences clearly marked. The flight path for the operation was indicated using coloured tape, and a collection of brightly coloured pins indicated the colours of the route marking flares that would be dropped by the Pathfinders.

Doug made his way to the operations blackboard, which took up almost an entire wall to one side of the room. The blackboard was divided into several sections. On the right-hand side was the date of the operation written into squares sitting above a drawing of the route into Germany that indicated the expected weather patterns. He took note of the expected prevailing wind patterns, knowing that it would have implications for the mission's timing over the target area.

The big Canadian then scanned the centre of the board where the names of each of the participating pilots were listed, along with their call code for the sortie. There, for the first time, was the name Bell. It was now official; everything that he had trained for over the last two years was going to be tested that evening. Feeling oddly excited to finally be going into action, Doug paused for a moment before surveying the rest of the information on the board concerning assignments, take-off times, and bomb loads. He took one last look at the description of the weather for the evening, paying close attention to the expected cloud cover on the flight in and over the target, and then turned back to the map that showed the anticipated flak areas.

Doug transferred the information to his chart, drawing the route to be followed and coloring in the flak defence zones. He then calculated the flight plan, including notations for each of the various stages of the flight and the directions in which the aircraft must be flown to offset the drifting expected due to the wind. This was the type of meticulous work in which he took great pride. The intricacies of the calculations provided a welcome diversion from time spent wondering about what the evening's action might bring.

The briefing over, Doug and Colin turned their attention to the next order of business – the mandatory test flight of the aircraft that would be their ride over Germany that evening. The two men donned their flight gear and were ferried out to the waiting aircraft. Standing next to their aircraft was the Sergeant in charge of the groundcrew who quickly took them through details for the plane and anything they should be paying attention to while taking it through its paces during the test flight or, as the Sergeant called it, the "sling round". Colin signed off that the plane was in working order and climbed aboard. Not long afterwards, the Mark XX Mosquito raced down the runway and surged into the air. For fifteen minutes, Colin put the plane through its paces, flying low over the English countryside while Doug familiarized himself with the local geography, tested his calculations, and opened and closed the bomb doors. Satisfied that the Mosquito was ready for action, Colin brought them back to Downham Market, landing comfortably and then taxiing to their designated spot in the assembly area.

"Everything is ready for tonight, Sergeant," said Colin, as he walked away from the plane.

"We'll have her shined up for you – complete with the gifts you'll be delivering to our friends over the Channel," came the reply.

The formal preparations now complete, Colin and Doug made their way to the Mess for a meal of bacon and eggs - standard fare, particularly prior to missions. Once the last of the eggs had been sopped up with bread and the final drop of coffee had been drained, the waiting began.

Two hours for an anxious aircrew can seem like an eternity. Never having flown into battle before, Colin and Doug could only imagine what they might encounter over Hannover that night. They quickly learned that too much idle time leads one to contemplate all kinds of nasty alternative endings for a sortie, so it was best to find other things to occupy one's mind.

Soon enough, however, the word came down to gear up in preparation to be driven to the airfield and their waiting plane. The two men quickly made their way to the locker area and climbed into their flying gear, checking harnesses, pulling on flying boots and jackets, putting helmets, goggles and oxygen masks around their necks, and tying up the tapes on their Mae Wests. After signing for their parachutes, they made their way out to join their comrades for the short ride to the assembly area. Doug quickly returned to the briefing room to retrieve his flight bag from the duty officer charged with guarding them until flight time. He surveyed the contents to ensure that all the tools of his trade (maps, log book, pencils, spare flashlights, and a plastic compass) were there. He also inserted the secret codes for the mission, including the details on radio frequencies, call signs, and flare colours for the evening.

Climbing into the truck, there was little conversation; each man was alone with his thoughts, dealing with the curious mix of excitement of taking to the air and the anxiety associated with heading into battle. It was at this point that the stress and strain on the airmen was at its highest level; take-off was imminent and each man was now fully focussed on what might occur in the coming hours. For a new crew on its maiden mission, Doug and Colin had only their imaginations to rely on, supplemented by conversations with other veteran aircrews who assured them that there would be a warm reception laid out by the Germans.

They arrived at their plane, KB 212, the Mosquito Mark XX that they would be relying on to get them to the target and then home again safely. The ground crew was doing last minute preparations for the flight, attaching the cables from the battery cart to the engines and wiping the windscreen down. The Sergeant they had spoken with earlier in the day met them with a smile. He handed Colin a clipboard holding RAF Form 700, the piece of paper to be signed by a crew prior to flight to certify that the plane had been worked on and was cleared for flight, including details on any modifications, repairs, or major servicing.

"Sign here, sir, confirming that you have received a plane that is in proper flying condition." Colin quickly scrawled his name on the form and handed it back to the waiting man.

"Try to bring it home in one piece, sir," the sergeant said as he pivoted away from the plane.

The two men looked at each other, Doug gesturing to his pilot to climb aboard. As Colin clambered up the small ladder extending below the cockpit, Doug patted the plane, quietly saying that he was confident she would get the job done.

Once inside, Colin settled into his seat and adjusted his gear, making sure that he was able to operate the plane while still having ready access to his parachute and, if need be, the dinghy located near his feet. Doug followed in behind, wedging himself into his spot in the cockpit. The navigator had no proper seat in the Mosquito and had to make do with a small bench that sat to the right and slightly behind the pilot. Being a big man, encumbered with his parachute, Doug had learned early on that his movements needed to be carefully choreographed given the fairly limited space within which he had to work. He quickly stored his navigation instruments in the receptacle, gathered the wooden board that served as his plotting table, and clipped on his charts.

Mosquito cockpit. Small opening on the right is navigator's position during bombing runs.

The two men then secured themselves in place, the two shoulder straps and the two side straps gathered together and locked in place with a pin. As they did so, they heard the entry door being latched from the outside. Now was the time for each man to attend to his last-minute readiness checks. Colin slid the small panel to his left open and yelled out "Contact!" Towards the tail of the plane, the man on the ground overseeing the battery cart echoed his call. The Englishman smiled and pushed the button for the port engine. Slowly the engine turned over, then burst into life. Colin repeated the process for the starboard engine and was pleased with the same result. Both engines were roaring, the initial telltale blue flames from the exhaust lighting the air and quickly dispersing thanks to the flame dampers.

As each engine warmed up, Colin increased the rpms, gradually at first, eventually reaching a level that would enable the superchargers, magnetos, and constant speed units to be checked. He then throttled back and said, "Everything checks with the engines, Doug. How are things from your end?"

"We are good to go," came the response. With the checks completed, Colin signalled to the groundcrew that all was ready and that the chocks should be removed from the wheels.

"Chocks away," came the call from outside the plane.

The same procedure had been repeated with each of the seven aircraft that sat in the dispersal area waiting for the signal to take-off. At last, the signal came that operations were a go. Slowly, in the declining light, each of the fully loaded bombers began to move from its dispersal pad, bouncing across the field at low speed. Adjusting the throttles, Colin taxied the wooden bomber along the line with the other aircraft, following the signals of the groundcrew member waving the two flashlights to head onto the taxi strip. "What's the first heading, Doug?" he asked in preparation for the imminent take-off.

Doug consulted his figures, double checking the course and time. "I make it one-nine-two," he said. Colin nodded and adjusted his compass. Doug then again confirmed that the gas gauges and the light switches were functioning properly, leaving nothing to chance.

The Mosquito slid by the blue and amber lights that marked the taxi strip until the plane reached the head of the runway where Colin brought it to a halt to await the okay to proceed. At the end of runway sat a caravan with a corporal and the aircraft control pilot whose job it was to phone the flying control officer to confirm when each plane took off. One by one, the Mosquitos roared down the runway, lifting off into the evening sky. Sitting in their cramped quarters, Colin and Doug waited for the green light to signal that it was their turn to go. At 23:10, they got the signal. Colin pushed the throttles forward, one notch at a time, the plane shuddering as the rpms increased. "Time to go through the gate," he said as he released the brakes and opened the throttles up fully. The Mosquito raced forward, the parallel strings of lights pointing their way to the unknown. The bomber bumped and rocked along the mile-long runway and, as the speed increased, Colin moved the control column forward to lift the tail, gradually easing the bomber into the air. Doug duly noted that they were airborne on his log sheet, while Colin pulled the undercarriage lever bringing the wheels up. As they rose, the pair donned their oxygen masks and Colin turned the plane on their initial course towards Hannover.

As they flew, conversation was limited. Colin focussed on controlling the plane, clutching the controls and monitoring the instruments in order to maintain the required height, speed, and heading. At the same time, Doug checked their heading, recalculating frequently in order to ensure that they would arrive at the required turning points at the designated times. As they concentrated on their respective jobs, both men pushed their anxieties deep into their subconscious.

Strato-cumulus clouds covered most of northern Europe that night between 15,000 and 25,000 feet. To the two men, it seemed that the sky was filled with alternating thick and thin layers of heavy clouds, with views of the landscape below seldom being available. Not surprisingly, the cloud cover would make it difficult for the aircrews to see the route marker flares dropped by the leading pathfinders as they tended to become rapidly obscured upon release. That put increased emphasis on the navigator to plot the way in using other means. As the planes neared Hannover, it became clear that the target itself was shrouded in thick cloud.

"Where are we?" asked Colin.

"Working on it," replied Doug, poring over his calculations. "We're getting close."

Any doubt about that was quickly alleviated with the initial thumps of anti-aircraft fire. For the first time in their lives, the pair saw the ominous, yet spectacular light show created by German anti-aircraft defences. Flashes of light appeared in the clouds, giving the impression that the plane was cruising above a lightning storm or a fireworks display. Red flashes expanded and then faded, quickly replaced by another burst. As they got nearer to the target, the plane was buffeted by the explosions, focussing Colin on holding the plane steady as it rocked back and forth.

"Christ, this is insane!" blurted out Colin.

Beginning with the first burst of flak, both men experienced the visceral reaction to uncertainty as their stomachs began to churn. Adrenalin heightened their awareness of their surroundings. Each successive explosion and its accompanying flash of light pummelled the aircraft, tossing it about as if it were weightless. Holding their breath, Colin and Doug fought to control the fear that seemed to well up from deep within their soul. With Herculean effort, both men refocussed and pushed the negativity that had been escalating aside.

"Hold on, Doug. This is going to be bloody rough," Colin grimly called out, gripping the yoke tightly as the plane bucked and bounced its way across the angry skies. "I guess we're not welcome."

"Wait a few minutes and see how they feel about us then," Doug replied.

The closer to the target area they came, the more the skies seemed to be bubbling with the murderous red flashes and thunderous bangs. By now, Doug had made his way into his battle station by crawling down into the nose of the plane to guide Colin in to the target and to aim and release the four 500-pound bombs carried in the belly of the plane.

"Three minutes to go!" yelled Doug above the din. He scanned the skies but saw no sign of the target indicators. Time seemed to stand still as he looked quickly from side to side in hopes of spotting the tell-tale glow of the flares. "I can't see anything in the cloud. What should we do?" he yelled, punctuated by the continued explosions in the vicinity.

The decision was quickly made to circle the target area – perhaps a sound strategic decision, but not one easily taken given that it extended the time that the plane was within the kill zone for the German guns. With each passing second, it seemed inevitable that a shell would eventually strike home. So intense was the shelling that the air seemed to be boiling.

With little to go on in terms of target indicators, Doug plotted them in based on time and distance from the last known point. While he pondered whether they had missed the target, a solitary target indicator flare dropped through a gap in the cloud right in front of them, a welcome ball of golden light that was backlit by the glow of fires from below. Through the gap in the clouds, Doug could now see enough detail to know that they were bang on target. Hannover was spread out ahead and to starboard.

For the first time, Colin and Doug were aware of searchlights springing to life. All around them menacing cones of light came together and then divided again, relentlessly slashing across the skies in search of the elusive bombers. From his vantage point, Colin watched the light show dance around the target area while Doug glued his eyes on the bomb aimer. Both men were now becoming aware of other lights joining the display. Flashes from the ground were now visible, as streams of red balls were reaching into the air; more concentrated fire was rising up from German guns. These were punctuated by the bursts of light from the bombs dropped by the leading Mosquitoes making landfall.

"Bomb doors open!" Colin yelled as he kept the plane steady through the turbulent sky.

His eyes fixed on the bombsight, Doug's whole world was concentrated on aligning the markers with the target. At last, the target appeared in his line of sight and the Canadian navigator squeezed the bomb release with enough force that he felt that his thumb would come out of its socket. "Bombs going!" he yelled above the din, and when the little light by the bomb switches went out, "Bombs gone!"

An odd moment of relief swept over the two men. They had done it – they had made their way across hostile skies, found their objective, and delivered the payload. They had successfully dropped their first bombs in anger. Below the plane, sticks of bombs floated across the target, followed by sharp, angry flashes of light below the smoke; intense, white bursts of light combined with slower yellow gleams, waving searchlights, and the continuing red bursts of flak. From his position in the nose of the plane, Doug now called out over the intercom. "Course out two-nine-one, two-nine-one!" He then realized that he was still desperately squeezing the bomb release, so he slowly and deliberately released the trigger. Colin pulled on his bomb release lever to ensure that the payload had been delivered, and then closed the bomb bay doors. As Doug climbed back up to his seat, the in-board camera whirled automatically to record the results. Now it was time to go home.

Slowly the Mosquito banked over, dipping one wing in a seeming salute to the smoke and fire that was Hannover. For the first time, the pair glimpsed the canal that lay beside the target area. The aircraft leveled off and set off towards the North Sea, England, and bacon and eggs.

"See anything, Doug?" asked Colin as he scanned the skies ahead of the plane for any indication of German fighter activity.

"All clear so far," Doug replied, craning his neck to view behind and above the Mosquito as they set their course for home.

As they flew, they were pleased that it had been relatively uneventful. "I suppose that expecting the worst is the best approach after all," mused Colin.

"If that was the worst that could happen, I feel a lot better about our chances going forward," replied Doug, still on the lookout for enemy aircraft. "Knock on wood," he added.

"What?" asked Colin.

"Knock on wood? Just something you say when you're worried that you're being over confident and tempting bad luck," he explained.

"I like that," said Colin, "must remember to use it more often".

Tempting the fates is never a wise decision. Not long after uttering words suggesting that life in a bomber over Germany was not too taxing, the operational inexperience of the two men raised its ugly head. Their flight path home was taking them over Emden, a German port that served as a major naval facility. As could be expected, it had its own formidable anti-aircraft defense systems in place. As the bomber made its way within half a mile of the city, shells began to burst in their flight path. "Who are they firing at?" asked Doug. A few seconds later, the answer became frightening clear – the gunners had gotten their range, warmed up their guns and were now accurately firing at the lone aircraft. Flashes and bangs bracketed their plane in a manner that was much more intense than they had left behind at Hannover; the smell of cordite hung in the air.

Colin and Doug were quite shaken by what was happening, but reacted quickly. Without hesitation, Colin put the plane into a panic power dive, dropping it from 25,000 feet to 10,000 feet in only a few seconds, the plane shaking and straining as it dove. With great difficulty, he used the elevator trim to arrest the dive, which now had the Mosquito below the flak bursts and flying at a speed that allowed them to race away from Emden physically unscathed but emotionally battered. The power dive had exceeded the known safety limits of the Mosquito, but KB 265 had responded well, just as they had hoped.

"Bit of a boob, that," lamented Colin as they sped out over water on their way back to Downham Market.

"I'll carry the can for that one – never thought that we'd still be a target even though we're heading home," responded Doug. "I'll pay more attention when plotting courses next time."

Maintaining strict radio silence as they flew, the two men conversed about matters of the day, the small talk helping to pass the time on the inbound route. "I don't care how much training you take, nothing could prepare you for that madness," mused Doug.

"I thought that the whole German army had us in their sights," agreed Colin. "I wonder how the others are doing?" With radio silence still being maintained, the two men stared out at the night, feeling strangely alone in the vast darkness.

With England visible in the distance, Doug flicked the switch on the IFF (Info, Friend or Foe) signal to alert those watching the skies that they were a friendly aircraft. Soon the air waves came alive as each of the returning aircraft sought landing instructions from the WAAF ground radio operators. For the weary aircrews, the angelic voices of the women on their headsets were a welcome relief from the previous hours' terrors.

After bumping along between the two rows of lights that outlined the runway and taxiing to the dispersal point between lines of feint blue glow, they were waved in by ground crew using their flashlights. As they deplaned, thoughts immediately turned back to their squadron mates. "Is everyone back?" asked Colin.

"A pair of white gloves this evening, sir," came the reply. Noting the confused look on the new crew's faces, the Sergeant explained, "All accounted for with you being the last to return."

Colin and Doug made their way to the mandatory debriefing with the squadron's "spy". The two men confirmed that they reached the target and dropped their bombs, a claim that would be borne out once the films were developed. They then reported any other matters that seemed unusual seen on the journey out, over the target, and on the way home. As it turned out, they had been the last of the flight to bomb the target and, through good fortune more than anything else, had delivered their payload on target. As a result, Colin and Doug were quickly hailed as a press-on crew who brought home their attack regardless of the German efforts to knock them from the sky.

As they made their way to the mess, the pair shared the view that their new reputation was quite unjustified, and made note of the things that they had learned from their initial trial by fire: #1 – important military installations could be more heavily defended than industrial targets; #2 – flying over such places when they were not targets was a recipe for possible disaster. As they sat down for a meal, Colin looked at Doug and said, "There is no substitute for experience in this business."

Karlsruhe – September 7th

After flying on the previous two evenings, Doug and Colin were not on the active duty roster and were able to stand down on September 7th. Flying over Germany on consecutive nights and at high altitudes had a way of wearing aircrews out. The combination of tension and anxiety, combined with the dehydration that occurred at high altitude, tended to sap the energy of pilots and navigators alike. As a result, the squadron liked to alternate its active crews to ensure that its personnel were as fresh as possible.

The squadron was still active that evening, with seven planes sent out to bomb the oil refineries at Karlsruhe, Germany. Bad weather at Downham Market meant that the returning planes had to be diverted to another airfield to land. When the day dawned on September 8th, Doug and Colin learned that one of the planes, flown by Flight Lieutenant Jake Jacobs and Flying Officer Hobbs, had crashed at RAF Bradwell Bay. While both men had survived, the story of their misadventure quickly made the rounds at the base.

On their return to Downham Market, Jacobs recounted the story to his compatriots. "With only the starboard fan going, I was told on no account swing to port! I landed right of the runway by the FIDO installation but the starboard engine would not shut down, so I pulled up the under carriage. Not being able to close the starboard engine throttle fully caused the aircraft to float, resulting in a wild ride through various huts, air raid shelters, and hedges. We ended up in a plowed field." (Blunt).

Hobbs recalled that as they descended, they "made a mess of it, bounced over the FIDO pipeline, through an aircraft shelter, a hedge, and a herd of cows, coming to rest close to what I thought was a small jetty by the sea." (Blunt).

The next morning, the aircrew, who were unharmed, went back to inspect the plane in the daylight and found that what they had thought was a jetty was actually the FIDO installation fuel tank containing thousands of gallons of petrol. If the thought of almost causing a major gas explosion was not shocking enough, more horrifying was the discovery that the airfield was lined with aircraft parked wingtip to wingtip, three deep across the runway on the port side of the crashed bomber. On the starboard of their Mosquito were four Warwick bombers, a farm house, the gap in the field they had plowed through, and another flight of Warwicks. They learned from the base personnel that their crash landing occurred amidst aircraft being assembled for the launching of *Operation Market Garden*, the massive airborne invasion targeting Arnhem in the Netherlands. The aircraft that they had narrowly missed on the wild ride were gliders and tugs preparing for the attack.

Nuremberg – September 8th

The next night, nine planes from 608 Squadron linked up with 36 other Mosquito bombers to attack Nuremberg, an important location for armaments production. Factories within the city developed diesel engines for submarines, Panther tank parts, motorcycles, and other armaments for the German army. In addition, the city was also a main railway hub linking the area to the rest of the country.

At 20:46, Colin and Doug lifted off and formed up with the other aircraft to make their way over Germany. "This will be a test of your skills, Doug, my boy," noted Colin, surveying the dense cloud cover laid out below the bombers as they flew over the continent. Visibility in the flight stream was good, and, to the relief of the aircrews, the skies were empty of enemy aircraft.

Doug slithered his way into position in the nose cone and prepared to guide Colin in for the bombing run. "Steady on, Colin," he called out, "I have a good view of the markers and we are bang on target."

The Mossie roared across the air space. "We are cricket free," smiled Colin, as he scanned the sky for any sign of fighters. Seconds later, his smile disappeared as light flak began to appear, with flashes and puffs of smoke ahead of the oncoming bombers. During the pre-mission briefing, Colin and Doug had learned that the Germans were employing a new wrinkle in their air defense system. Some of the German anti-aircraft guns were armed with shells that contained the same colours used by Bomber Command to mark targets. By detonating them above unoccupied areas, the Germans hoped to divert the attacking planes and have them drop their bomb loads miles from the intended targets, a practice known to Allied aircrews as "spoofs".

As they approached Nuremberg, what appeared to be two red Route Targeting Indicators burst at about 18,000 feet far to the port side of the aircraft. "What do you make of that, Doug?" asked Colin of his navigator.

"According to my calculations, we are dead on line with the target," he replied. "If I'm reading my charts correctly, those markers are some 20 miles away from our intended destination."

"Bloody spoofs, then! Well, we shall press on and ignore them," said Colin, confident as always that Doug was bringing them in precisely where they needed to be and exactly on time.

Within minutes, the bombing runs commenced with each successive Mosquito dropping its ordinance to good effect, blanketing the area around the target markers. As they turned to make their way home, Colin and Doug gazed down at the city below. Two large fires were visible, the glow from which continued to seen for 100 miles on the return flight.

Berlin – September 11th

Doug and Colin sat together as Group Captain Kyle outlined the action scheduled for that evening. "Gentlemen, our ten planes will be joining up with several of our brother Mosquito squadrons to make a concentrated diversionary raid on Berlin," he began. The assembled aircrews looked at one another, acknowledging that the evening's festivities were going to be challenging. "I say diversionary because the main target for the 226 Lancasters from 5 Group tonight will be the railroad installations at Darmstadt. You lot will join with 37 other Mosquitoes from No. 8 Group to launch a raid on Berlin designed to draw some of the attention away from the big boys as they make their strike some 300 miles to the southwest. For the record, this is the first time that Darmstadt has been targeted."

Kyle then turned the briefing over to the base meteorologist to provide the current conditions over the continent. "You can expect to experience moderate cloud cover over Berlin, likely strato-cumulus topping out at 8,000 feet." The briefing then moved on to details on target marking, with the assembled crews being told that the target indicators would be green and red for the mission.

That evening, Doug and Colin would be flying a Mosquito Mark XXV that had been constructed in Canada. That alone created a sense of pride within the Canuck navigator, but the occasion was made more auspicious for it being the first time a Canadian-built Mossie was to attack Berlin. Colin could sense the importance of operation to his navigator, Doug looking more grimly determined than ever. Eight hours later, they were winging their way to the German capital.

As the planners had hoped, the Germans focussed the lion's share of attention on the marauding Mosquitoes, with fighters rising into the bomber stream beginning some 50 miles from the Reich capital. Adding to the stress of possible night fighter attacks, the aircrews were now being subjected to active searchlights, beginning in the Frankfurt-Mainz-Mannheim area, followed by the ever-present concentrated lights over Berlin itself. For 300 miles, the incoming Mosquitoes bobbed and weaved their way through the bright beams that slashed across the sky. In the cockpit, the dormant feelings of fear reappeared. Never completely forgotten, the level of apprehension that accompanied the possibility of being coned in the penetrating lights served to amplify each man's level of concentration.

As they prepared for the final approach, Doug noted the absence of the predicted cloud cover. "We have clear skies running in."

"We also have visitors in the area," called back Colin, having spied telltale signs of night fighters. "The goblins are on the prowl!"

As they neared the city, the fighters backed away and left the defence of the city to the guns below. Bursts of heavy flak seemed to be everywhere as the bombers bore down on the drop point. Searing flashes of red morphed into dark ominous smoke as the planes raced towards the target. "I've got the markers in sight," called Doug. "Keep her on the current heading."

"Doing my best, just bags of flaming onions to avoid. Hold on. I've got green and red markers to the north!" called out Colin.

"Spoofs for sure; stay the course," came the reassuring response from the navigator.

Moments later, KB 235's bombs rained down on Berlin, followed by flashes and smoke as they struck home. Colin banked the plane away from the fires visible below and scanned the skies for the return of the fighters. As they flew, Doug spied an explosion to the port side, followed by what looked like flaming debris. "Oh God, no," he said, realizing that one of the inbound planes had been hit by a flak burst. "Can you see anything, Colin? Anything at all?" As he looked towards his partner, the usual grin had been replaced by a hard stare.

"They're gone," is all he said.

In a millisecond, two men's lives had been ended.

Neither man spoke, just stared ahead, contemplating what they had seen.

Two and a half hours later, their Mosquito safely home, the pair made their way to the debriefing session. As they entered the hall, Doug glanced at the chalkboard, looking for the dreaded word "missing" beside one of the aircraft. The board was clear. "Everyone is accounted for," he said, breathing a sigh of relief. Stepping outside and glancing over the fens, he thought about the plane that had gone down and the men who had been on her.

"At least our boys are home safe," said Colin as he walked up beside him.

"Yes, we all get another night," replied Doug, as he turned and walked into the darkness.

Berlin – September 15th

Since their initial attack on Hannover, Colin and Doug had put the lessons learned that night into practice on five more occasions with attacks on Hamburg, Nuremberg, Brunswick, and the two visits to Berlin. After only two weeks of combat flying, the pair had gained experience with the dangers of anti-aircraft fire, evading circling German aircraft, and bobbing through the probing beams of searchlights, all of which were the price of doing business in the skies over German cities and industrial areas. The two men quickly learned that the German shells, accurate, deadly, and difficult to avoid, were more dangerous than the propeller driven fighters that were considered lucky if they were able to get near a Mosquito. With flak, it was just a matter of chance whether you were hit and, if so, what damage might be wrought on you personally or on the aircraft itself.

As frightening as it had been on their initial sorties, flying over Berlin was infinitely more dangerous. Any aircraft attacking a German city could expect a warm reception, but when the target was the capital city of the Third Reich, there was a particularly impressive defense system to be penetrated in order to press home an attack. The city was ringed by what seemed like thousands of anti-aircraft guns, all of them guided by ground-based radar and coordinated by a rangefinder and an analog computer. Most of these guns were the formidable 88 millimetres that could fire between 15 to 20 rounds a minute each, with their 20-pound shells able to reach up to 39,000 feet. When a battery of these were targeted on a plane and firing, the resulting explosions and withering spray of shrapnel were lethal. If that was not enough, smaller calibre guns filled the skies with streams of baseball-sized projectiles capable of slicing through the plywood aircraft like a hot knife through butter.

And yet, there was more than just the guns that had to be respected. The formidable defense network also included radar-controlled searchlights. Given the size of Berlin, the phalanx of searchlights extended across the entire urban area – perhaps for 20 miles, lighting the skies brighter than any Hollywood premiere. For a plane to be caught within the cone of the lights meant a terrifying flight as the Mosquito passed from one cone to the next as it flew across the city. Even at 25,000 feet, being bathed in the white/blue beams of light could be disorienting. The light entering the cockpit made it difficult to see, reflecting off all surfaces which, in turn, often created a false horizon. Pilots would struggle to confirm that the aircraft was indeed in a straight and level position. Given the width of the light beams, it was very difficult for a Mosquito or any other bomber to escape back into darkness. It was not uncommon for pilots to adopt a corkscrew-like flight path under full power, like a large trout trying to shake itself loose from a fishing hook, to avoid being successfully bracketed by the lights.

As Colin and Doug approached the target, they were coned by searchlights. Instinctively, Colin began taking evasive action, leaving it to Doug to direct them over the target using only dead reckoning, as it was difficult to discern any identifiable landmarks on the ground. Doug quickly calculated their position by using a previously fixed position against known or estimated speeds over elapsed time and course.

"Two degrees to port!" he called over the intercom. Now back on course, they began their run in over the target. Without warning, there was a colossal bang as a shell burst directly below the plane. The force of the explosion jolted the ten-ton Mosquito straight up, filling the plane with the sickening odour of explosives.

Time seemed to stand still as the two men rapidly scanned the plane and themselves for any telltale signs of damage. "Are you all right, Doug?" gasped Colin as he checked his instruments.

"All good … as far as I can tell … but that smell is bad," he struggled to respond, his breaths coming rapidly, his senses overwhelmed by the smell of cordite that filled the plane.

"That is the least of our worries," said Colin, as he stoically informed his partner that the explosion had stalled both of the plane's engines.

"What are you going to do now?" asked the usually unflappable navigator, his sense of dread rising as he realized that they were now gliding, powerless over the heart of Berlin.

"We wait," was the response from Englishman, "what else can we do?"

Although anxious about their situation, Colin knew his aircraft well. Merlin engines had gravity-fed carburetors and he hoped that the sudden rise in elevation had merely interrupted the flow of fuel to the engine. Seconds seemed like a lifetime, but the engines quickly sputtered back to life and the greatly relieved crew pressed on with their bombing run.

"That's a sound I have grown to love," muttered Colin as the hum of the restarted engines mixed in with the thumps and bangs of the exploding shells.

Moments later, after successfully releasing their bomb load, the abused Mosquito sped away from Berlin with the two men ever watchful for the possibility of fighters.

"You aren't frightened are you, Doug?" asked Colin as his navigator clambered back to his bench for the flight home.

"No – I'm bloody terrified."

After landing at Downham Market, both men became aware of their exhaustion as the tension and adrenalin drained from their bodies. As he began the deplaning process, Doug shifted his weight towards the ladder below his seat. As he moved away from his position in the cockpit, Doug noticed a hole the size of his thumbnail in the floor of the plane below where he had been sitting. Puzzled, he then spied a corresponding hole in the cuff of his pant leg. Upon further inspection, he found a similar hole in the collar of his flight jacket and another puncture in the roof of the plane's fuselage. "Good God!" he thought, "that was too close for comfort."

As the pair stepped off the plane, they both looked towards the tail of the aircraft where the force of the blast had been concentrated. To their astonishment, they saw that the rear of their Mosquito resembled a colander, with the entire frame of the aircraft peppered with perforations. Stunned that nothing vital to the plane's ability to fly had been severed by the shell fragments, they turned to each other in amazement. "This is bloody dangerous!" noted Colin.

The next morning, Colin returned to their plane for a further look, arriving just as it was being towed away for repair. The Sergeant who oversaw their groundcrew approached him. "I have a present for you," he said as he dumped a handful of shrapnel into Colin's palms.

"Where did this come from?" Colin queried.

"The crew found it in your parachute ... the one you were sitting on."

Downham Market - September 16th

Over a span of less than two weeks, the two men had been gifted with battle experience – no longer were they the green flight crew struggling with doubts and apprehension over what lay ahead on any given mission. Like all those around them who had flown before, they had learned that fear was their constant companion; a companion that had to be controlled. It was an unspoken truth that fear could be a killer.

The previous day, as the Wing Commander announced that the target would be Berlin, Colin had been surveying the room and noticed a new crew in attendance. It was clear that the intended target had visibly shaken the two men. Colin looked at Doug and pointed to the two men across the room. "They look petrified," he said. As the navigators assembled to go over their calculations, it became clear to Doug that his fellow navigator was indeed anxious to the point of being non-functional.

Heeding Colin's suggestion that he should help if he could, he approached his colleague and offered his assistance. At the same time, Colin approached the shaken pilot and spoke quietly to him, reassuring the man that everything would be okay. The good-natured Brit soon realized that his words were having little impact, as the frightened pilot kept repeating, very quietly, "We are not coming back from this, *I know!*"

Colin thought nothing more of the conversation, his focus being on his own responsibilities and the rather harrowing flight that he and Doug had experienced the night before. It was not until the morning of the 16th that it all hit home. Colin learned that the crew that had been so obviously scared prior to the flight had not returned. He spoke quietly to Doug about his view that fear had contributed to their deaths. "It was bollocks to send them to Berlin on their first attack," he lamented, although he knew that he had no power to affect the outcome. Doug nodded, both men having accepted that every night required a maximum effort and that there was no room for doubt. Every man in the squadron knew that they had an obligation and duty to strike the enemy, whatever the cost. And that cost could be severe.

A Brief Respite

After their harrowing run into Berlin, Colin and Doug did not fly again that month, having been granted leave for the first time since arriving at Downham Market. For Doug, his first official leave afforded him the opportunity to reacquaint himself with a British family that had put him up upon his initial arrival in Scotland on July 19, 1944.

At that time, having disembarked from the "Empress of Scotland", Doug had been sent by train to Innsworth, England, to the Personnel Receiving Centre. Upon arrival, he and the other new personnel had filled out a form indicating

Bloody Terrified

their preference for locations in England where they would be paired with an English family and enjoy a week of disembarkation leave. Ten days later, Doug had been sent to Boston Spa, in Yorkshire, England, to spend a week with the Heydon family.

Boston Spa was a small village northeast of the City of Leeds. As he stepped off the train, Doug was approached by a young boy. "Are you Flight Lieutenant Redmond?" the youngster asked nervously.

"I am," responded the big Canadian, grasping the boy's hand in a firm hand shake, accompanied by a broad grin. "And you are?"

"My name is Michael ... Michael Heydon. I am to bring you home."

Doug picked up his bag, surveyed the station, and turned back to Michael. "Lead on, my friend." The pair made their way off the platform and walked towards the nearby taxi stand, the newly arrived navigator towering over his guide as they climbed into a waiting cab.

A short time later, the driver pulled to the curb and announced they had reached their destination. Doug quickly paid the man and climbed out, catching a glimpse of Michael racing up the stairs into the house. Seconds later, a middle-aged man limped outside and waved. Grabbing his bag, Doug made his way up the stairs.

"Flight Lieutenant Redmond. I'm Frank Heydon … please call me Frank," he said as he offered his hand.

"I prefer Doug. Pleased to meet you."

Frank Heydon was a British Army veteran who had been wounded in action earlier in the war and subsequently discharged. He was now living in a quaint home with his wife, Doris, and his youngest child, Michael. He soon learned that there were two other children in the family: a daughter, Denise, who was in the Women's Land Army, and an older son, Reville, who was a Sergeant Pilot. A few weeks before Doug's arrival at their home, the family learned that their oldest son had gone missing over the English Channel.

From the moment he arrived, Doug was welcomed as a member of the family. The Heydons included Doug in everything they did, touring the Boston Spa area, going to market and church, and enjoying evening games and conversation by a warm fire. Doug felt that, in some ways, he was filling a gap in their lives. It almost certainly filled a need in his life as well, as growing up in a small rural community had instilled the importance of family in his life.

When the time came to make his way to Downham Market, the family invited him to spend his future leave time with them, if he so wished. Without hesitation, he thanked them for their generous offer and said that he would see them as often as he could. And he did, as he spent all of his leave time during his tour of duty with the Heydons. So important was it to him that he frequently wrote to his wife, Hazel, telling her of his time in Boston Spa.

As September came to an end, Doug and Colin had endured their baptism by fire, having completed seven missions, three of which were over Berlin. They had experienced the uncertainty and terror of flying through the dark skies over Germany, and had learned the importance of teamwork in getting the job done. Most significantly, they had begun to develop their survival instincts.

For the squadron as a whole, September had been a difficult month. Three Mosquitoes had been lost, two to fighters and one to anti-aircraft fire. Two others had been damaged by enemy action, and two more were damaged by non-operational accidents. For a period of time near the end of the month, 608 Squadron was down to only six operational aircraft. As troublesome as this was, it was the loss of two aircrews that had the greatest effect on the base personnel.

Ian Redmond

Chapter 6

October 1944 - School's Out

Brunswick – October 2nd

Autumn had arrived in RAF Downham Market. The daily temperature began to drop, making the never-ending dampness even less tolerable. Colin and Doug had not flown in thirteen days owing to their leave and several days of inclement weather. Their brief holiday from action, however, came to an end on October 2nd with orders to participate in a nine-plane raid on Brunswick. Taking off in the early evening, the Mosquitoes made their way over the target in under two hours, bombing with little opposition, a welcome respite from previous sorties over Berlin.

As they made their way home, discussions turned to the physical and mental demands of bomber operations. "Cripes, Colin, I don't know about you, but those last few flights knocked the stuffing out of me. I felt like I had been in a prize fight with Joe Louis."

"I'm not sure I would pay to see that," Colin laughed. "You're right though; this is bloody stressful work. It's only after the adrenalin wears off that I realize just how worn out I am!"

Indeed, bomber crews knew too well that the tension associated with attacking heavily defended targets, combined with the need for constant vigilance against German fighters and the dehydration associated with high altitude flying, was a constant drain on their energy.

Colin, in fact, had begun a practice that was designed to restore some of that energy. Once the target had been bombed and the Mosquito was safely away from the target area, he had determined that, by trimming the plane to fly at a consistent height and speed, he could take a cat nap. A key part of the process was an understanding with his colleague that, should anything untoward happen, Doug should awaken him immediately. "At the very least," said Colin, "make sure to rouse me well in advance of our return to base so that I can bring us home. That, after all, is one of the duties of the navigator."

Not surprisingly, this practice provided Doug with a heightened view of his ability to fly the plane. Having had some previous training, the navigator was emboldened enough to believe that he could do both jobs simultaneously without difficulty.

"Colin, rise and shine – time to bring us home."

As the plane cruised over the Channel, Doug took enormous pride in having safely brought them to this point, but recognized that navigating was a far cry from piloting.

"Damn, I was in the middle of a beautiful dream," replied Colin, smirking at his colleague as he took the control stick. "And, you weren't in it."

It was Doug's turn to smile.

Downham Market – October 3rd

They had the night off. Without hesitation, the decision was taken to leave the base for an evening of relaxation with good food and drink. It was late afternoon when the two men cycled their way into town searching for a brief respite from their duties as an operational bomber crew. Having made arrangements with a local to look after their bicycles (a necessary precaution in that they were difficult to come by and, if left unattended, had a nasty tendency to go missing), the pair settled on the Crown Hotel for refreshments. Having found a table and ordered some food, Colin made his way to the bar to order the requisite ales.

"Evenin', squire!" called the man behind the bar. "Not on ops tonight, I see. Goin' to miss the show in Kassel, I hear."

Rather than respond, Colin simply took the drinks and made his way back to the table, feeling quite perplexed by the brief interchange.

"You look like you swallowed a spam sandwich. What's going on?" enquired Doug.

"It's probably nothing, but the barkeep told me that the boys are hitting Kassel tonight. How does he know that?"

"Someone has been very careless," replied the navigator, pointing to the poster hanging above the bar - *Careless Talk Costs Lives*. "It seems that not everyone is following those wise words."

"Well, I, for one, will be making a complaint to camp security. It would be bad form to have a spy in our midst relaying information to Germany," stated Colin as he sipped at his beer. "Doesn't it bother you, Doug?" he asked.

"Of course, but it doesn't sound like he was pressing you for information or confirmation. Just idle chat. That being said, it's still worth reporting. People need to be more careful."

Colin had come to learn that very little seemed to ruffle Doug's feathers. A calmer and friendlier man he had never met. As they ate, Colin asked Doug about his training days, hoping to better understand his partner's demeanour. Lingering over their meal, Doug recounted a few stories that were above and beyond what one might expect to experience during basic training.

"Similar to our situation here, in operational training, there were 32 men, equally divided between pilots and co-pilots, who were expected to sort themselves into two-man aircrews," began Doug. "In the group was a pilot from New Zealand who was a holdover from a previous class," he continued. "His plane had crashed on a training flight and his navigator had been killed. He approached me with the idea of crewing up, but we didn't seem to click, so he eventually paired up with a friend of mine named Watkins."

"Not every match is made in heaven," chortled Colin.

"You have no idea how prophetic that comment is," responded Doug. "Shortly after crewing up, their plane failed to return from a training run. Later that day, Watkins arrived back at the station and told the authorities that as they reached 25,000 feet, the New Zealander opened the hatch and jumped out of the plane. Thankfully Watkins had already completed a tour of duty and knew how to control the aircraft, managing to stabilize it long enough to allow him to jump clear."

Goldfish Club Shoulder Badge (Source: Author's collection)

"Good God! Why would the pilot bail out?"

"It seems that his goal was to achieve the most caterpillars in the Royal New Zealand Air Force. Apparently, he had already killed two navigators and, with this occurrence, had destroyed three Mosquitoes."

"What happened to him?"

"He was found out and taken away. I am sure he's in some private hell dedicated to idiots."

Caterpillars were awards given to those that survived a crash through the use of a silk parachute. Similar awards were provided to those that survived crashes over water by using a rubber dinghy, the "Goldfish Club", and those who escaped captivity on land, the "Boots" Award.

"I'm glad that I didn't receive a caterpillar," said Doug. "I think that being a member of the *Goldfish Club* is enough for one man."

"You crashed over water?" asked Colin incredulously.

Doug's broken watch showing the time that his plane hit the water (Source: Author's collection)

"Yes," came the reply. "On May 7, 1943, I was the navigator on an Anson on a training flight that went down in the Gulf of St. Lawrence. I spent almost six and a half hours in a dinghy before being picked up," he said, pausing briefly to sip his beer. "Sadly, only three of us were saved. Our wireless operator died."

"Bloody hell! Here's to your wireless operator ... and to the dinghy," offered Colin, feeling somewhat blessed to be flying with a man who had already gone through difficult situations and who continued to do so without hesitation.

"Cheers, my friend," said Doug with a smile. "We'd best be collecting our bicycles and heading back to base."

"Cheers," came the response, complete with a clinking of the near empty glasses.

Cologne – October 10th

Shortly after 10 a.m., Colin and Doug were informed that they were to participate in that evening's mission. After a few hours of playing bridge with some of the other aircrew, Doug made his way to the briefing, where he and the other ten navigators selected for the mission learned that they were heading to Cologne.

That evening, they sat on the dispersal area, waiting their turn to take off. At 18:10, the third aircraft in line raced down the runway and lifted off. Seconds later, the Mosquito's port engine failed and it crashed into a field near the end of the runway. It had become known that the Packard Merlin engines on the Canadian-built bombers had an issue with connecting rods when the pilot pushed the engines to their maximum on take-off. On this occasion, as Flight Officer J.A. Smith accelerated into the air, the connecting rod broke and penetrated the engine casing. Smith immediately feathered the engine. As the plane was only 100 feet in the air, there was no ability to jettison either the bombload or the fuel in the drop tanks. Without hesitation, Smith opted for a belly landing.

The crews waiting in line watched helplessly as the Mosquito bounced back to earth, grinding its way across the field until coming to a stop not far from the Officers Mess. At that moment, the Station Medical Officer was in the Mess enjoying a pint of beer. Hearing the crash, he raced outside to offer assistance, beer in hand. As he approached the downed aircraft, Smith, an Australian, grabbed the beer, downed it, and then climbed out of the plane. "Thanks Doc," he said as he surveyed heavily damaged plane.

Five minutes later, Doug and Colin lifted into the air, flying over the downed bomber. The show must go on.

Berlin – October 27th

The Mosquito was quiet. The two men were exhausted from the evening's efforts, having once again flown into the cauldron that was Berlin and delivered four 500-pound bombs onto the designated target.

"That's six times we've hit Berlin in our first sixteen flights," muttered Doug as he returned to his seat alongside Bell. "It feels like twice the effort than other cities."

"Indeed," said Colin. "I can think of a few things I would rather be doing … well, one anyway," he said, shooting Doug a sly wink.

Doug had charted their way home, taking into consideration their earlier lessons and ensuring that their return flight was over open countryside, away from other areas ringed with anti-aircraft defences. As was now his custom, Colin trimmed up the aircraft to fly straight and narrow and closed his eyes for a brief nap.

"Keep an eye open for anything amiss, Doug," he said, before drifting off. Doug sat quietly, his eyes darting about as he monitored height, air speed, direction and, equally importantly, the telltale signs of enemy aircraft. With Colin gently snoring, the Mosquito cruised along at a constant speed at 25,000 feet. After the hell of Berlin, the inbound flight was shaping up to be more relaxing.

No white lights were on to indicate night fighter radar contact, and the skies were clear. The red light glowed dully indicating that the plane was being tracked by ground radar but, in Colin's view, that was standard operating procedure. He had previously indicated that one could expect to be followed until the plane cleared German airspace. For Doug, it seemed like an idyllic moment to just survey the heavens and let the tensions of the just completed mission evaporate. In moments like this, thoughts turned to the beauty of the skies, the boundless horizons, and the freedom that flight provided. Deep in thought, Doug quietly monitored progress as the plane sailed along. Suddenly, and without warning, there was a thunderous bang below the starboard engine, accompanied by a bright flash and the acrid smell of cordite.

Doug unleashed a single word, "Fuck!"

Colin's eyes popped open, completely confused by the sudden wake up call. He looked at his partner, noting, for the first time, the evidence of fear in his normally calm navigator's demeanor; his knees were visibly shaking.

Fighting the rocking and wobbling of the bomber, the pair realized that an anti-aircraft shell had narrowly missed them. "Where the bloody hell did that come from?" cried Colin as he deftly steadied the aircraft.

"I have no idea," replied Doug. "According to the map, we're flying over open countryside. There is nothing marked on the charts about guns in this area."

Now fully awake, alert, and very anxious, both crewmen surveyed the plane to see if there was any damage. Expecting further shelling, Colin took the plane up a few thousand feet in an effort to upset the calculations of the gun crews below. Strangely, no further shells came their way, and they continued home, puzzled by the experience and relieved to still be in the air.

As their heart rates returned to normal, Colin looked at his navigator. "Did I hear you swear?" he gently needled his flying companion.

"Shut up!" came the emphatic reply. After a brief pause, the two men began to laugh. Once again, they had seemingly cheated death.

Upon return to home base, the Mosquito touched down lightly and Colin taxied them to their allotted spot. As they left the plane, both men peered up at the fuselage expecting to see significant damage. Seeing only a few small punctures, Colin looked at Doug. "Did I dream that whole incident?" he pondered.

"If you did, then we were both in the same dream."

The two men told their story to the station spy during the required debriefing. Recounting the exact route of their return flight, they quickly learned that they had been picked up by a solitary radar installation that tracked them for several miles. Their steady height and constant speed were relayed to a local Wehrmacht training centre for anti-aircraft teams comprised of women. The school was only allocated one shell per day for practice purposes, and a plane travelling on a straight line at a constant speed and elevation was a practice opportunity too good to pass up.

"They'll never know how close they were to graduating at the top of their class," said Colin, smiling through slightly clenched teeth.

"I don't plan to give them a chance for a second test," replied Doug, as he marked the location of the school with a red circle on his charts for future reference.

As the month drew to a close, Colin and Doug had logged another 11 sorties into Germany, with a combined flight time of 40 hours and 25 minutes. Of those 11 flights, four targeted Cologne and three were to Berlin. The pair had now flown a total of 18 missions; unofficially graduating them into the world of experienced aircrews.

The squadron as a whole had flown 225 sorties during the same time frame, 217 of which hit the primary target, with only 6 flights aborted. While success rates remained high for the squadron, the costs continued to mount; three more aircraft had been lost, as well as two aircrews.

Ian Redmond

Chapter 7

November 1944 - Breathe

As the calendar turned to November, the Allies were closing in on the Germans in the Netherlands and were soon to drive the enemy out of the Scheldt Estuary and Belgium. For Bomber Command, efforts to destroy the German capacity and determination to fight intensified as the month progressed.

After 57 days of active duty, Colin and Doug had flown 18 missions against targets deep inside Germany. Their levels of pre-flight anxiousness had diminished with each successive flight as they learned to rely on their respective skills and the capabilities of the aircraft. No longer surprised by the intensity of enemy counter measures, both men had found a way to subdue their apprehensions. Yet the cold grip of fear was always nearby, dormant but easily rekindled without warning. Aircrews could only focus on those matters that they could manage. There was little value in worrying about whether luck was on their side on a given flight. Colin, for his part, did not dwell much on the possibility that their luck might run out, preferring to focus his attention on things that he could control, understanding the details of the next raid and flying the aircraft. Doug, too, kept his mind occupied on other things, applying himself, with meticulous detail, to the principles and practices of navigation and his single-minded goal of guiding Colin precisely over the target at exactly the desired time, accurately marking it for the bombers that followed them.

For others in the squadron, November began with a bang. Flight Lieutenant Lockyer and Flying Officer Sherry saw their first mission of the new month begin, and end, quite quickly. As their Mosquito raced down the runway, Lockyer throttled back the engines in an attempt to abort the take-off. He was able to straighten the plane and get it parallel to the runway, but their excessive speed, combined with the wet grass, left him unable to slow the aircraft's momentum. Inside the cockpit, the two men stared straight ahead as the bomber streaked across the perimeter of the airfield and into the neighbouring darkness.

At the edge of the airfield, just past the perimeter track, sat the Radar Hut. On this evening, the Officer on Duty was a Canadian named Campbell. As per his duties, he was watching through the cupola in the roof of the hut as each plane lifted off. As he watched the navigation lights of Lockyer and Sherry's incoming Mosquito, he calmly pulled the blinds closed and dove for cover. The aircraft struck the hut with a resounding thud, the jarring impact knocking both men unconscious with Lockyer's face hitting the steering column and Sherry's bouncing off the bulkhead. As the men regained their senses, they struggled to extricate themselves from the plane, emerging undamaged save for the loss of a number of teeth. Sherry realized that the ringing in his ears was actually the high-pitched whine of the instrument panel gyros. Stumbling away from the downed aircraft, a new sound struck his ears. "I became aware of a continuous stream of profanity in a Canadian accent. I discovered later that this flow of virtuoso swearing had been coming from under the debris of the wrecked radar building some 60 yards in our rear." (Blunt)

When the pair returned to active duty several weeks later, they were greeted with the kind of good-natured ribbing that their fellow airmen loved to dish out. When it became known that the loss of front teeth and swollen gums had given Lockyer a pronounced lisp, it was only a matter of time before one of the women in the Control Tower was presented with a unique opportunity to dole out some particularly unsympathetic commentary. Returning from their raid over Germany, Lockyer and Sherry, flying in a bomber whose call sign for the sortie was S for Sugar, approached Downham Market. When they called in to announce their return, the melodious voice of the on-duty WAAC welcomed them. "Hello Eth for Thoogar," called the voice on the radio. "Your turn to land ith number thikth". (Blunt). There was always time for a good laugh.

Of greater concern was the fact that, for the second time in under a month, a 608 Squadron bomber had experienced a catastrophic malfunction. It was now abundantly clear that the issue needed to be addressed. Following a thorough investigation, the decision was taken to replace the faulty engine part in each of the squadron's Mosquitoes. When Wing Commander Alabaster announced the results of the study to his assembled flight crews, he was asked by a number of men how long it would take to be completed.

"Three months," he replied calmly.

"What do we do until then?"

"You'll continue to fly operations," came the authoritarian response.

Knowing that Alabaster occasionally flew on missions, he was pointedly asked what he would do if his engine quit on him on take-off. "I would die like an officer and a gentleman," came the reply.

Hannover - November 9th

Two a.m. was an unusually late hour for a sortie into Germany. Even for an aircrew accustomed to flying in the early morning, two in the morning was generally the time when Colin and Doug would have been making their way back home after completing their bombing run or settling down for a post flight meal and coffee, complete with rum. On this cold November morning, however, the pair sat patiently waiting for the green light that would signal them to speed on their way. As they sat, conversation turned to the food package that had been delivered to them prior to entering the aircraft.

"Did you look in the bag, Doug?"

"No, I just asked what it was ... spam sandwiches again," he noted with disgust. "I just jammed the bag into my pocket."

It was always the same. As they made their way to the ladder, someone would invariably present them with a paper bag containing something for them to snack on to keep their energy up during the long flight. Spam. An American concoction whose basic ingredients were alleged to be pork with ham meat added, salt, water, sugar, and sodium nitrite, the latter included as a preservative - a preservative so effective that if one were to open a can 75 years after it came off the production line, it would still be as inedible as it was when first produced. Topping off this culinary delight was a natural gelatin that formed during the cooking process.

"We have been at this for two months now. Have you ever eaten one of those godforsaken sandwiches?" asked Doug.

"Good Christ, no! Isn't it enough that we have to face the Nazi guns each night? Why would I take on any more risks than that!" The two men laughed, before being interrupted by the glow of the green "go" signal.

"Onwards and upwards," said Colin, as he throttled the engines to full power and the bomber hurtled down the runway, lifting into the air well clear of the hedges that lined the end of the tarmac. Doug gave Colin the coordinates and he quickly set course for Hannover. As usual, the pair donned their oxygen masks as the plane climbed to its prescribed cruising altitude.

About an hour had passed when Doug glanced over at Colin. The pilot's head was nodding towards his chest. Doug, who was accustomed to Colin taking short naps during missions, was puzzled by the fact that Colin had not told him to take control and wake him if needed but, even more odd, was the fact that he was napping on the outbound portion of the flight.

It was then that Doug noticed that the plane was not flying straight and true. It was, in fact, turning slowly and decreasing in height. "Colin!" he yelled, shaking the pilot's shoulders. The only response was a tilting of his colleague's head backwards, eyes still closed. Doug quickly grabbed the steering yoke, struggling to gain control of the plane. Levelling it out briefly, he released his grip and grabbed the emergency oxygen bottle that was strapped beside him, near the observation bubble at the front of the plane. Turning on the flow of oxygen, he reached over, quickly removed Colin's mask, and began to wave the bottle in front of his pilot's face. Looking somewhat like a contortionist, Doug attempted to revive his pilot while at the same time trying to keep the bomber from ploughing into the ground below.

As the plane continued its now increasing descent, Colin's eyes flickered, eventually opening and looking directly at Doug's face. The first thing he saw was the oxygen bottle. He grabbed it and sucked deeply, drawing in the life-sustaining gas. Within seconds, he retook control of the aircraft, stabilizing its height and lessening its speed. While having been unconscious for less than a minute, in that brief terrorizing time, the plane had dropped from 25,000 feet to close to 10,000 feet.

"Where are we?" queried Colin as he tried to clear the cobwebs from his head. "And why were you at the controls?"

"Let's just say you picked a helluva time to take a nap!"

Doug's quick thinking and immediate actions had averted certain disaster. Now, as they cruised along at the lower altitude, he discovered the cause of the distress. Colin's oxygen line had malfunctioned and he had experienced hypoxia, a potentially fatal condition where the body's oxygen supply is cut off. Without a functioning oxygen supply, both men knew that they could not continue on to the intended target, so Colin turned the Mosquito around and Doug set the course for Downham Market.

Upon landing, the duo met with the Intelligence Officer and laid out the evening's events. Neither man ever spoke of their adventure again. Colin, for his part, would often say that Doug was a first-rate navigator - in his view, the best in the squadron - and that he was lucky to have him as a partner. While Doug was never a pilot, on this particular day, he earned his wings.

Hannover - November 21st

Not having flown again since their oxygen mask misadventure, Colin and Doug's return to action found them once again sitting in their bomber at the ungodly hour of 2:30 in the morning. "It's some cold out there tonight," remarked Doug.

"Could be worse, I suppose," countered Colin. "At least there is more heat in here than in the bloody hut!"

When their time came to lift off, they bounced their way down the runway and once again climbed into the air. Colin pulled the lever to retract the landing gear and adjusted the rpms of the engines. Changing course as they climbed, the aircraft turned and headed on its way over the Channel.

Fifteen minutes into the flight, Colin's attention was drawn to the oil pressure gauge on the starboard engine.

"We're losing pressure on the starboard side," he called out. A quick glance confirmed the situation.

Colin engaged his microphone. "DO, this is K for Kilo requesting clearance to return to base."

"K for Kilo, this is DO. What is the nature of your situation?"

"We're losing pressure on the starboard engine. Not going to be able to continue."

Within seconds, instructions were given to abort the mission and to return to base.

Once again, the two men returned home having not been able to deliver their payload to its intended destination. As they stood beside the plane while the groundcrew began its examination, Colin suggested that perhaps they were not meant to visit Hannover any more.

Castrop Rauxel - November 21st

Fourteen hours later, Colin and Doug found themselves once again in line, waiting for the go signal. As their earlier plane was still being repaired, they found themselves once again in Mosquito KB 347, the aircraft that had presented them with the oxygen supply surprise. Assured by the groundcrew that the system was now properly functioning, Colin signed off

Form 700, shinnied on board and strapped himself in, adjusting the parachute that acted as his seat cushion and tucking the dinghy between his feet.

On this night, the pair were flying as the lone Mosquito ahead of a larger formation of 230 Halifax and Lancaster bombers targeting the synthetic oil plants at Castrop Rauxel. Unlike previous sorties, Colin and Doug were to make their way to the target using the GEE radio navigation system, a system that was based on the measurement of the time delay between two radio signals to determine the position of the plane, designed to facilitate night bombing.

It was Doug's job to monitor the signals through the use of the GEE box that was installed in the cockpit. The box was exactly that, rectangular in shape, closed save for a single opening that was fitted with a padded tube. The two transmitters sent out signals that appeared on the interior black face of the box as green blips. Navigators were charged with comparing the blips against lines on a specific map that they carried on GEE flights.

Doug rested his face against the opening and turned the two knobs to tune the receiver to the two GEE stations. Immediately the blips began to appear. "Got 'em, Colin," he said as he pulled his face away to record the readings and mark the results on his map. Measuring the time delays of the signals and cross referencing these numbers on the gridded lines on the chart (the grid giving the system its name – GEE as in grid), the former lumberjack could determine their position in space, known as taking a fix. Where the two lines crossed, that was the position of the aircraft.

Doug's attention was solely on monitoring the blips from the radio stations and then translating the results to the charts. GEE was known to be an accurate means of navigating and Doug was confident that he would be able to bring the attacking fleet of aircraft directly over the desired target. Before doing so, however, he had one more duty to attend to that would, if deployed properly, serve to confuse the German air defence scheme. On the floor of the fuselage, just below his feet, were bundles of foil, nicknamed "Window".

Simplistic in its design, Window was comprised of individual strips of foil, twelve inches long by 1.5 inches wide, that were piled in bundles of 2,000 strips. When employed, Window created a cloud of reflective foil that would show up on German radar as a blip, approximating that of a heavy bomber. For the German air defences, the sudden appearance of multiple images on their screens caused immediate confusion and made radar-controlled interception of the bombers very difficult since radar operators could not differentiate between the real aircraft and the phoncy readings. Night fighters operating with their own radar, homing in on what appeared to be an enemy aircraft, found themselves flying through skies filled with swirling screens of tin foil. Even the

Lancaster deploying Window

ever-present searchlights began blindly probing across the sky, unable to cone on an actual bomber. The inability to pinpoint the attacking planes meant that anti-aircraft guns were randomly firing into the sky with no sense of where their targets might be.

On a Mosquito bomber that was ordered to deploy Window, it was the role of the navigator to physically toss the foil out of the plane. As the plane approached the designated

Window release point, Colin tapped Doug, indicating it was time to get prepared. Doug nodded his head and slid off his bench, taking up his accustomed position on his hands and knees, his head in the bubble in the plane's nose.

On the floor immediately in front of him was a raked chute that was held in place by a spring-loaded flap. Doug opened the flap and awaited Colin's signal to deploy the foil strips. "Now!" came the word from above. Doug reacted immediately, reaching back and dragging the bundle of foil strips towards the chute. Even for a strong man like Doug, accustomed to cutting and hauling timber, getting the bundles into position as quickly as possible had him puffing and panting with the effort. Not only were the bundles heavy, the process was now made additionally difficult by the frigid air that was rushing through the chute into the plane. Doug pushed each separate bundle through the opening, dealing with the piercing cold air that quickly numbed his fingers. As each bundle tumbled out of the plane's nose, the bomber's slipstream created a powerful suction that pulled the bundles apart and sent the individual strands of foil cascading into the night air like a blizzard of silver confetti. The last bundle disappeared through the slot and Doug snapped the flap closed.

"Window away!" he announced. Having done their job, content that the radar operators on the ground were now frantically trying to interpret the sudden appearance of a large number of enemy aircraft, Colin affected a course change to bring the Mosquito on line for the real target.

Returning to his bench, Doug immediately jammed his hands into his armpits, having learned during his days in the woods in the winter that the quickest way to warm one's hands was to get them as close to the body's core as possible. When his hands were sufficiently thawed, Doug returned to his position in the nose and began the process of bringing the plane onto the target.

Doug and Colin in Mosquito KB 347 take to the sky heading for Castrop Rauxel (Source: Andy Moore)

Window had done its job. Both the fighter opposition and the anti-aircraft fire were light, providing only a minor distraction for the crew as they bore down on Castrop Rauxel. Doug's familiar baritone voice filled the cockpit. "Thirty seconds," followed by, "Bombs away!" The plane shuddered with the release of the bombs and rose slightly, now 2,000 pounds lighter. The automatic camera shutter clicked as bright flashes appeared on the ground. "Take us home, Colin" he said, as he again dragged himself back to his seat. Not needing a second reminder, Colin banked the plane and sped away from the target area which was soon to be severely battered by the following host of heavy bombers.

Downham Market - November 22nd

Having flown twice on the previous day, Colin and Doug found themselves with a down day. By noon, they had attended to their duties and quickly decided that it was the perfect time to make their way into town to share a pint and chat about whatever topic presented itself. Downham Market, as always, was warm and welcoming and, for Colin at least, it presented the opportunity to spend some time with his wife. The plan was to share a few moments with their fellow air crew before Colin would beg off to join his wife for dinner.

They arrived at their favoured watering hole, the Crown Hotel, where they were joined by one of the Dutch crewmembers, Flying Officer O. H. Terrell Guyt, who had successfully graduated from being known as Buddy to the now more familiar Harry. Over the course of the afternoon, Harry regaled his colleagues with the tale of how he came to be part of 608 Squadron. As he explained it, at the outset of the war he had been a pilot with the Dutch Air Force, but was shot down within a few days of the hostilities beginning and taken prisoner.

"That must have been hell – a prisoner of war. How did you adjust?" asked Colin.

"And how did you get here?" added Doug.

Harry smiled and drew a healthy mouthful of his ale. "It was not so bad at first," he said. "I was released by the Germans within a few days. We were allowed to go home on the understanding that we would not take up arms against them again."

Rather than rejoining the military, Harry took the decision to fight the Germans in a different way; he joined the resistance. "It was not a long career," he continued. "I was caught once again." Pausing for another sip, his features hardened. "This time there was no leniency … this time I was taken by the Gestapo." After interrogation, the Germans sent him to a camp as a slave labourer working on railways.

He told his fellow airmen about the camp conditions and being worked beyond the point of exhaustion. "I was quickly getting weaker … the will to live was leaving me." At this point, the story took an unexpected turn. "I found myself working in the hospital assisting one of the doctors, a German man, whose family had been mistreated by the Nazi authorities prior to the war. I befriended him," he went on, taking another long drink and setting his empty glass down. "One day he told me that if I could get myself admitted to the hospital, he might be able to get me out of the camp. When I asked how to do that, he said it was up to me to find a way." Nearing physical breakdown and wanting to escape before he would no longer have the ability to do so, Harry made the kind of decision that only the desperate would entertain. That day, as the train bringing the new prisoners to the camp arrived, he placed his foot on the track as one of the cars passed him. Within seconds, the wheels had removed all the toes from his foot.

"Good God, man!" blurted out Colin.

"It was an easy decision," he continued. "I could not go on. And it had the desired result."

Once admitted to the hospital, true to his word, the German doctor managed to spirit him out of the camp, where Harry once again connected with the underground. This time, they aided his escape from the country, which eventually brought him to England. As a former airman with the Dutch Air Force, it was not long before he joined the RAF as part of Bomber Command, assigned to 608.

Harry stood, put on his cap. "I have to get back to camp. Thanks for the drink," he said, then turned and walked away with only a slight limp. Doug and Colin watched as their comrade-in-arms left the hotel, wondering if they would have made the same decision.

Nuremberg – November 25th

The test flight was done. Doug and Colin made their way to the mess hall for their pre-flight meal. As they walked, they quietly discussed their orders for the evening.

"It seems that we are in the first wave of tonight's action," said Colin, acknowledging that they, along with 11 other 608 Squadron crews, had been tasked with hitting Nuremberg, while a second wave of 39 Mossies from other squadrons would arrive over the same target some three hours later to inflict more damage. A further 18 Mosquitoes would be attacking Stuttgart, Erfurt, and Hagen to create diversions from the main target.

"Bit of a role reversal tonight with the big boys dropping Window in support of us for a change, eh, Colin?"

"Let's hope they don't cock it up!"

A few hours later, the two men boarded Mosquito KB 298 and went through their final preparations. At 21:45, the green light blazed and the word came down. "C for Charlie, you are cleared for take-off." Within minutes, the twelve planes crossed over the English Channel, soon to be joining up with 27 other Mosquitoes to strike Nuremberg, the center of the Nazi regime. Weather over England had been fair, with largely moderate visibility. As the planes flew over France and into Germany, the bombers entered into thick medium and low cloud.

"It looks like our friends in the Stirlings and Liberators have done their job," said Colin, as he scanned the night skies for fighter activity. "I see no evidence of any company up ahead."

"None behind either. I take back most of the bad things I have said about them in the past," replied Doug with a chuckle.

The flight gods were indeed kind on this night, as the German fighters reacted strongly to the feint attacks and Windowing. The main force of Mosquitoes came on completely unopposed. Equally fortuitous was the change in weather that found Nuremberg cloud-free for the first wave of attackers - not only cloud free, but searchlight free as well.

Doug took to his familiar position in the nose of the plane. As they neared the target, he was astounded by the sight below. "We have caught them with their pants down!" he cried out, staring in disbelief at the target area completely ablaze with lights. As if the Germans now realized their error, the city lights suddenly extinguished, replaced by the glow of the target indicators as the red and yellow star bursts lit the night over the northwest part of the city. As Doug counted down to the release of their payload, the city lights came on again, providing a perfect view of the target. "Bombs away!" he yelled.

One by one, the following Mosquitoes attacked. The ideal conditions had resulted in an excellent concentration of bombing in the city's built-up industrial area. Colin and Doug circled over the target to take photos of the results. As they watched, they were mesmerized by the pattern of concussions on the ground as each successive bomb blast looked like expanding ripples in a stream. The two men were quickly snapped back to reality as the telltale signs of anti-aircraft fire began to appear in the bomber stream.

"A bit like closing the barn door after the horse has got out," mused Doug.

"What was that?"

"It means ... never mind. Just get us home."

Duisburg – November 30th

Pathfinder squadrons were often equipped with the OBOE navigation system, an RAF-developed mechanism that exploited Allied radar technology as a means to facilitate effective night raids over Germany. OBOE utilized a combination of radar pulse signals emanating from two designated stations on the southern coast of England that would be picked up by receivers installed in the aircraft.

One signal measured the distance from each station to the target. This signal would be heard by the pilot, whose role it was to maintain the plane along the arc of the signal that would eventually pass over the target area. The second signal was a letter indicating where the aircraft was on its way towards the target. Informed by basic geometry, the system used the known distance to the selected target as the radii of two separate arcs of a circle, measured independently from each station, one tracking the bomber. The intersection of the two arcs was considered to be the accurate bombing release point.

In practice, the process began during mission briefings, when aircrew would be given a longitude and latitude point ten minutes flying time from the target - the "switching on" point. Each crew were given a time to be at this point. Five minutes before reaching the switching on point, the navigator would listen for the plane's individual code that signalled the turning on of the transmitter.

Once on, an invisible electronic beam was created that ran from the switch-on point to the target, the location of the aircraft in relation to the beam being indicated to the pilot by either dots (meaning that the plane was to the left of the beam) or dashes (the plane being to the right of the beam). If the pilot heard a steady sound, it meant that the plane was on beam. The exact position of the bomber would be calculated when the crew heard the first letter on the beam. The switch-on point was A, a quarter of the way to the target was B, halfway was C, and three quarters was D. Once the bomber was settled on the beam, airspeed and height had to be maintained. When the pilot heard the D signal, a steady note, sounding remarkably like an oboe, would follow. When that note was cut, bombs would be released.

OBOE had proven effective in operations in the Ruhr Valley but, as attention shifted to Berlin in 1944, the system had produced diminishing results. In response, the RAF tested changes to the process that would provide the sought-after results on longer distance flights.

On November 30th, Colin and Doug led a flight of 18 Mosquitoes aimed at marking Duisburg's tar and benzol plant (two important components of synthetic oil) for a major raid involving 576 Bomber Command aircraft. Apart from targeting an industrial site of strategic importance, the attack also provided an opportunity to test the ability of OBOE to guide multiple aircraft on a single radio frequency channel.

On this particular mission, the planes flew two abreast, with Doug and Colin in the first pair, flying Mosquito KB 406 (code named K). Each succeeding pair flew close behind those immediately in front of them, although at a slightly lower altitude in order to avoid the slip stream of those in front. Radar in England monitored the aircraft, managing to keep them on track at the pre-determined place and time. The Mosquitoes flew into France, heading over the Somme, where they turned east and sped into German airspace over the Ruhr Valley.

The major raid was supported by several diversionary tactics, including a Mandrel Screen and Windowing over Holland. Mandrel Screens were produced by aircraft fitted with an antenna array in the nose of the plane. Flying in a line, patrol aircraft fitted with the antennae would aim signals at the German Freya and Wurzburg early warning radar installations, scrambling the systems' readings. For the planes heading to Duisburg, the combined efforts of the diversions caused great confusion for those directing the German interceptors onto targets. As a result, the inbound Mosquitoes and the following heavy bombers experienced little in terms of interaction with fighters.

Over the target, cloud cover was thick, albeit at lower altitudes. Above the clouds, the night was lit by a full moon, providing good visibility for the attacking aircraft. Colin and Doug approached the bombing point from 26,000 feet, releasing their bombs based on OBOE ground marking that provided a red glow visible through the clouds. Within seconds, the second Mosquito released its payload, followed seconds later by the next pairing of planes. The overcast conditions did not afford the crews with a view of their work, so they turned away without any sense of the level of success of their initial efforts. They knew, however, that following behind was the bulk of the bomber force that would deliver the main blow on the industrial sites below.

Upon return to England, the individual crews were debriefed. Remarkably, the entire flight of Mosquitoes had released their bomb loads at essentially the same time and, more astonishingly, the subsequent analysis of photos taken the next day showed an error of only 25 yards. Those same images showed the destructive might of Bomber Command. The priority factories of Heiderrheinische Hutte and Kabelwerke were severely damaged, as was the neighbouring railroad station. The main tracks and sidings showed numerous hits, as did the associated bridges and railroad yards.

For Colin and Doug and the other 608 Squadron aircrews, the results provided an enormous sense of pride in terms of their skills and their tenacity when leading a major raid.

As November came to a close, Colin and Doug had another 10 missions to their credit. Their confidence in their abilities and in the performance of their aircraft had grown, as had their reputation for getting the job done. As evidenced by their role in the Castrop Rauxel raid and the attack on Duisburg, they were getting tapped to take on important roles on a more frequent basis.

November had been a busy month for the squadron as a whole, with another 223 operations flown with the loss of three aircraft and three others damaged. The squadron continued to pay a price for its actions, with another three men falling as casualties.

Ian Redmond

Chapter 8

December 1944 – Weave! Weave!

Since September, Bomber Command had dropped 163,000 tons of bombs on German targets, an astronomical increase in comparison to the 40,000 and 8,000 tons during the same three-month period in 1943 and 1942. (Frankland, 1970). Based on these numbers alone, there can be no disputing that Bomber Command was increasing its contribution to the combined Anglo-American bomber offensive.

Indeed, the combined efforts of the RAF and the USAAF were putting increasing pressure on the German war machine. In particular, Germany was facing a crisis resulting from the devastating effectiveness of Allied air operations against targets involved in the production of oil. Albert Speer, the German Minister of Armaments, warned Adolph Hitler that the shortage of oil was threatening to shut down the country's surviving industries and hamper the mobility of its armed forces. Speer was of the view that the situation would continue to worsen if Germany's air defences were not improved.

While Speer lobbied for refocussing resources on combatting the Allied air offensive, within Allied circles a debate was raging over the most effective means of bringing the war to an end. Air Chief Marshal Sir Charles Portal, the Chief of the British Air Staff, advocated strategic bombing of industrial targets. Recognizing the dramatic effect that the bombing of synthetic oil facilities was having, he maintained that the best course of action for expediting the end of hostilities was the continuation of industry-focussed attacks. He bolstered his arguments with references to the Germans having lost access to the small oil fields dependent on the synthetic oil plants operating within their borders, in his mind, it was clear that a concentrated effort against in Poland and the larger ones in Rumania due to the advancing Russian Armies. Concluding that the Nazi war machine was left almost wholly these plants was the key to victory.

Air Chief Marshal Portal

At the same time, Air Chief Marshal Sir Arthur Harris, in his role as the Commander-in-Chief of Bomber Command, was advocating a significantly different approach. In his view, the general aerial bombing of major German cities was the more effective path to victory. He argued that a limited focus did not always produce the expected results, relying heavily on previous experiences when Allied attention was paid to ball bearing plants, only to discover that said plants were not as important to German military efforts as had been anticipated. Harris believed that with German armies virtually defeated, a campaign based on bombers ceaselessly attacking major cities was the key to achieving victory. This view had been the basis for *Operation Thunderclap*, a bombing campaign that aimed to destroy major German cities and break the resolve of the German people to resist.

With the arrival of December, the debate had been renewed, with the discussions ultimately centred on whether the priority was to be the bombing of oil facilities or cities. While it was recognized that cities had often been bombed because weather conditions precluded a more targeted attack on specific industrial objectives, they had not been singled out as the focus for a strike. The sense that victory was within reach had altered the arguments to provide greater consideration of whether strategic bombing or military occupation would be the more effective means of securing the desired end of the war. For those who favoured occupation, bombing was viewed as subjecting the German people to needless devastation, which could in turn make relations between the occupying forces and the general population more difficult. Furthermore, in major cities, wanton destruction would make many areas impassable for ground troops. If the intention was to rely on mobile armed forces to secure and maintain peace, the thinking was that Bomber Command should refrain from the *Operation Thunderclap* approach.

Harris, for his part, certainly favoured attacking the cities. A review of the statistics for the last three months of 1944 show that Harris continued to focus Bomber Command's activities on major cities. In fact, during that time period, 53% of the bombs dropped on Germany fell on major cities, with only 14% on oil facilities. Even more telling were the October numbers, where 66% of raids were on cities, as opposed to only 6% on oil plants. (Frankland, 1970). Portal continued to press Harris to refocus on the German oil industry. Even though Harris was far from convinced that such an approach would lead to a quicker resolution, he did increase the number of attacks on oil installations in November.

Air Chief Marshal Sir Arthur Harris

Unbeknownst to Portal and Harris, Albert Speer had written to Adolf Hitler in early November noting his concerns with the situation in the Ruhr Valley, the industrial heartland of the Third Reich. In his message, Speer indicated that the situation in the Ruhr had reached what he felt was a critical stage. In particular, he noted that many industries in that geographic area had been directly damaged by the bomber offensive, with the remaining factories and plants unable to access the necessary raw materials to sustain their outputs due to the destruction inflicted on major transportation hubs, rail lines, and canals.

Speer wrote to Hitler again in January of 1945 providing a particularly grim assessment of the impacts of Allied bombing on German oil production. Speer informed the Fuhrer that in comparison to normal production rates for a month (about 284,000 tons of aviation, carburetor, or diesel fuel), December saw only 151,000 tons produced. Most striking was the reduction in aviation fuel production, down from a normal yield of 197,000 tons to a mere 25,000 tons. (Frankland, 1970). The reduced production, combined with depleted stockpiles and the unlikelihood that the damaged plants could be repaired, led Speer to vociferously register his complaints about the need to better defend German industry.

While the overarching strategy for conducting the air war was a principal concern of RAF leadership, the rationale for why a particular target was favoured over another was of little concern to the Allied aircrews. The only concern for the men of Bomber Command was to follow their orders, taking care of the things that they could control. The where and when were for senior commanders to determine.

For 608 Squadron, December would see a slight shift in priority targets to a greater emphasis on industrial areas. It would also see them taking on a different role, supporting military operations in response to a German offensive in the Ardennes.

Ya Anglichahnin!

The war on the ground was now impacting the war in the air. With each passing day, the Wehrmacht was being pushed back into Germany. On the Eastern Front in particular, the Russian juggernaut was driving forward at a rapid rate, steamrolling its way towards Berlin. Bomber Command was watching these developments very closely, recognizing that, with Berlin a frequent target for long-distance bombing raids, the potential existed for downed bomber crews to come in contact with the Russians. For the crews flying from Downham Market, a new choice presented itself for situations where a Mosquito was badly damaged in a sortie over Berlin; a crew could try to limp their way home to England, or they could opt to fly eastwards and parachute into Russian-held territory.

Choosing to follow the latter course was not without some uncertainty. While Russia was part of the Allied forces, their army was not predisposed to taking prisoners. For a downed Allied aircrew landing in Russian territory, there was a very real possibility that they would be shot since the

Russians were unlikely to be able to distinguish between a member of the RAF and a German, or not be interested in taking the time to so do.

In an effort to address such a potentially dangerous encounter, Colin, Doug, and the other Mosquito crews were given a small Union Jack flag that was to be pinned to their tunic and unfurled should the aircrew find itself on the ground east of Berlin. The flag was to serve as the first means of identifying the holder as a friendly. Each man was also provided with a leaflet that outlined brief instructions to be followed in the event that contact was made with Russian allies. The first - and perhaps most important - instruction, was learning a simple phrase that would identify the airman as English. If contact was made, one was to say repeatedly, "Ya Anglichahnin," (I am English), while raising one's hands, one of which should contain the flag. Crews were cautioned, however, to not attempt to extract the flag if they were spotted before taking action to prepare for contact, relying on the simple phrase to keep things relatively calm. Even so, senior commanders knew that this alone would not guarantee safety, but it was hoped that it would protect the pilots and navigators until such time as they were interrogated by competent officers and their stories could be verified. As an aid in such an interrogation, the leaflet also contained Russian writing that translated to, "Please communicate my particulars to British Military Mission Moscow."

In addition, each man was also supplied with a booklet that provided useful phrases in French, Italian, German, and Spanish for downed aircrew to be used to seek help from the general population.

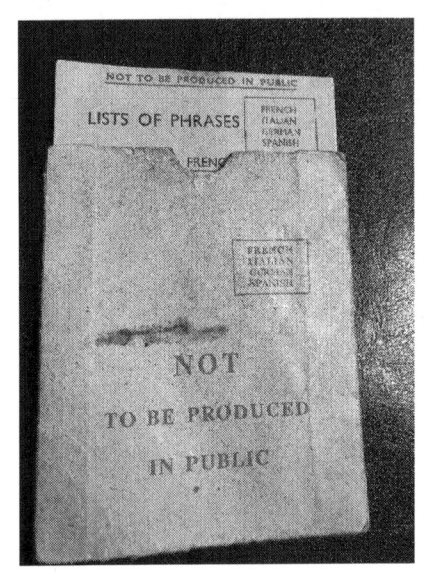

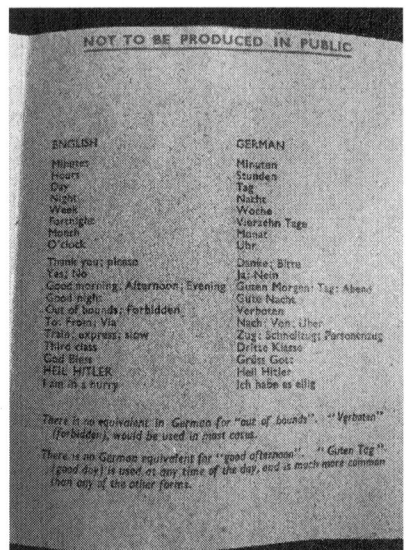

RAF Phrase Book for Downed Air Crew
(Source: Author's Collection)

For those crews who were shot down and found themselves in German-held territory, the situation was also changing. The German reaction to downed aircrews was becoming increasingly hostile, particularly for Mosquito crews.

It was not uncommon for surrendering airmen to be shot rather than taken prisoner. In response, each member of a 608 Squadron Mosquito crew was issued with .38 Smith and Wesson revolver, complete with 12 to 18 rounds of ammunition. Each man was under orders to wear it on all flights over German occupied territory. The understanding was that in the event of being shot down, aircrew were to follow Winston Churchill's creed of "Take at least one with you."

Duisburg – December 8th

The usual morning routine was cut short on this day. Rather than the twilight/early evening sortie, the selected aircrews were alerted to the fact that they would be flying an early afternoon mission. For Doug and Colin, this was only the second time that they had experienced a daylight flight since joining operations in September.

During the morning briefing, Wing Commander Alabaster had informed his men that the day's mission was an afternoon assault on the coking plants and gas furnaces associated with the coal mines in Duisburg. Not only was the squadron expected to fly in daylight, it was also going to be flying in the snow. The weather was overcast and heavy snow already blanketed the airfield. In order to meet their orders to attack the designated target, the runways would need to be cleared as quickly as possible. Once the aircrews were notified of the day's action, the order came down for all base personnel to report to the parade ground. As they arrived, each man was given a shovel and sent to work alongside the snow-plows to clear the tarmac for the day's operations. For the Canadian contingent, it felt like being transported back home where, growing up, they had spent countless hours scraping, pushing, lifting, and throwing snow. As they cleared the field, some rambunctious men sought to start a snowball fight. While good intentioned, it was quickly snuffed out. "Hey, you lot, save yer energy for fighting with the Nazi bastards!"

Within an hour, base personnel had sufficiently cleared the runways. For the aircrews, it was time to cool down, get some food, and then get into their flying gear. At the appointed hour, the aircrews climbed aboard the trucks to be transported to their planes. As soon as the trucks stopped, each pilot quickly signed off the necessary form and climbed aboard their planes as the snow swirled around them.

Having completed their system checks and finding everything to be in order, Doug and Colin sat staring at the rapidly falling snow. "Not to worry, Doug. There is no way that they will allow us to take off in this," said Colin. "I can barely see beyond the nose of the plane." Feeling confident in his analysis, he adjusted his parachute/seat cushion, content in the belief that he would be climbing out of the plane in short order. "Chin up, old man. In a few minutes word will come down that we're not on, and we can go somewhere warm and dry for a drink."

"Warm and dry, eh? Won't be heading to our huts then," laughed Doug.

As was usually the case though, the military doctrine of SNAFU (Situation Normal, All Fucked Up) was to reign supreme. Colin's prophetic words were incorrect; the green "go" light flashed on.

"Of course," he muttered. "Here we go then".

Colin nursed KB 350 down the recently cleared airstrip with heightened awareness, fearing that the bomber might slip and slide on its run out, unceremoniously dumping them in the fields beyond. Colin used every bit of his accumulated skills to control the wooden wonder as it accelerated rapidly and lifted into the air at what he hoped was a sufficient distance from the end of the runway. Quickly ascending in an effort to get above the clouds and the falling snow, the squadron formed up at 27,000 feet and made its way to Duisburg.

The rest of the flight followed the usual routine, although the usually omnipresent flak was somewhat lessened from previous sorties. More unusual for aircrews used to night operation was the absence of searchlights - not that this made things any easier. The anti-aircraft batteries were still being guided by radar and were still delivering enough high explosive rounds in the vicinity of the aircraft to keep flight crews on edge.

As the planes neared the English coast on the return home, the true impact of the snowstorm reared its ugly head as, one by one, the returning planes were diverted to other airfields. Downham Market was down for the day. For Colin and Doug, this meant they would be spending their evening with colleagues at RAF Upwood, home to the Lancasters of the No. 7 Squadron, some 32 miles southwest of their home base.

Having landed and completed their debriefing, the pair were given temporary quarters, after which they availed themselves of the local cuisine - the ever-popular bacon and eggs.

Wiesbaden – December 16th

Colin and Doug were now well acquainted with their extremely stressful and frequently perilous lifestyle. Both men had adjusted to the physical and mental demands of flying and had accepted the constant level of concentration needed for hours required to fly sorties deep into Germany. The pair had learned hard lessons, including the fact that airmen had to not only fight the enemy, but also a hostile environment in which they might encounter many kinds of adverse weather conditions. Occupational hazards such as strong winds, heavy cloud cover, lack of oxygen, frostbite, and lower pressures at high altitude meant they needed equipment to keep them warm and breathing and able to do their job.

The objective for this night was industrial facilities near Wiesbaden. The two men were fully prepared for the mission, having gone through the thorough briefing, tested the aircraft's air readiness, and gathered their thoughts for what the evening would bring. As they sat in the cramped confines of their plane, the focus was on the process of getting airborne.

"Seems to be taking longer than usual to get us on our way," noted Colin, as he checked his instruments for what seemed like the twentieth time since climbing into his seat.

"Maybe the war is over!" chortled Doug.

Minutes later, the intercom crackled. "Operation scrubbed – weather over the target area is impassable."

Colin glanced at Doug, "And so we stand down." Doug smiled as the nervous tension he had been suppressing suddenly dissipated. The trap door opened and the groundcrew drew out the small ladder to allow the men to deplane. As their feet touched the earth again, both men felt strangely deflated. They had put all their efforts into preparing for the evening flight, and now it was all for naught.

"You'd think I would be happier about this," said Colin as he pulled off his goggles and helmet. "But I suppose that can be rectified with a good beer."

"I have the same feeling," replied Doug as he pulled his navigator bag out of the plane. "All that work for nothing. And then we will do it all again tomorrow."

As they stood, the groundcrew began their work. "Stop yer belly-aching!" came a voice from behind. "At least you can have a meal and a drink somewhere warm and cozy. I've got to take the damn bombs out and drain the fuel tanks in this miserable climate!"

Feeling somewhat chastised, the two men joined their fellow aircrew mates and piled into the truck to take them back to dispersal. It was time to enjoy the unexpected night of safety and comfort before gearing up to do it all again.

Downham Market - December 25th

Christmas Day dawned on RAF Downham Market. Rather that the usual hustle and bustle of preparation for sorties into enemy territory, the air base was oddly calm. As was the RAF custom, no operations were scheduled on this day; instead, flight crews and base personnel were given the time to mark Christmas in their own way.

For those who were interested, Christmas morning began with a traditional carol service. As was his wont, WC Alabaster joined his men for a hearty sing along, happy to have a moment to share good cheer and glad tidings with each of the men and women who called the airfield their home. "Come on, you lazy lot, let's hear you!" he yelled before breaking into a rousing version of "Hark the Herald Angels Sing."

Following the singalong, the afternoon passed quickly as preparations were made for a traditional Christmas dinner. Unlike other nights where the Mess staff prepared and served the meals, Christmas afforded the opportunity for the enlisted personnel to enjoy being catered to by the squadron's staff officers and other non-commissioned officers.

As the throng assembled, Colin and Doug joined the other "servers" to dole out the evening's hearty meal. Gone was the usual steak and eggs, replaced by a slightly more lavish selection of food. As each man came through the line, they were presented with an entrée of soup, ladled out in a somewhat less than professional manner by a smiling Flight Lieutenant. This was followed by a succulent helping of roast turkey, complete with stuffing, brussels sprouts, and creamed potatoes.

The generous portions of food were washed down with copious amounts of beer and other drinks. Boisterous, good-natured conversations filled the hall as the assembled personnel took advantage of the opportunity to ridicule the base's contingent of officers. Once the main course was cleared away by the "serving crew", the meal was capped off with a traditional Christmas pudding, along with an assortment of cheeses, biscuits, and apples. After a few more ales to complete the meal, the soiree wrapped up with satisfied personnel making their way back to their abodes with the air filled with songs and laughter. For one day, the war seemed so far away.

Frankfurt – Dec 28th

The good feelings of Christmas seemed like the distant past as Colin and Doug prepared to board the truck to take them to their plane for that evening's mission. The assembled air crews went through their pre-flight routine. Pockets were emptied of anything that might inform the Germans of the squadron or aerodrome from which the plane originated should they be shot down. Once done, parachutes were gathered, and headgear and goggles were put on.

Once again, the truck deposited them at their waiting plane, where Colin signed the necessary paperwork and smiled his usual grin when told to try not to break it. Once inside and locked in, the countless repetitions of routine took over, each successive action blending into the next. For many, these were moments of déjà vu, progressing through the checklist having become second nature to them. For others, the last few moments before flight provided the opportunity to watch the sunset or the birds circling over the fens, a semblance of normalcy and calm to counterbalance what would be coming in the not-too-distant future.

Earlier in the day, they had learned that fourteen planes from 608 Squadron would be joining 73 Mosquitoes from other squadrons for a massed raid on Frankfurt. It had been 17 days since their last flight and the pair was champing at the bit to get back into the game. As had become his routine, Doug had spent a few days with the Heydons, helping to replace the family he missed in Canada before returning to the base for the Christmas celebration. Colin had enjoyed the company of his wife during the down time, a welcome respite from the toils of war. Refreshed and eager to get on with it, both men turned their focus to their unique responsibilities.

Since the outset of their partnership, the pair had assumed clearly defined roles while in the air. Colin, as the pilot, flew the aircraft throughout the operation and co-ordinated his actions with that of his navigator. He was the captain of the aircraft, responsible for their lives and the aircraft whilst in the air. If an emergency evacuation of the aircraft was necessary, the pilot had to stay at the controls and be the last to leave. The navigator was responsible for keeping the aircraft on course at all times, reaching the target and then the home base. He had to maintain a high level of concentration for virtually the whole of the flight, anywhere from 3 to 4.5 hours. He also filled the role of the bomb aimer.

And, in Doug's case, he occasionally acted as an alarm clock on flights home.

Colin had started and tested the engines and was now waiting for a signal from the control tower for take off. At 16:30, the green light was given and Mosquito KB 406 raced down the runway and into the air. Less than two hours later, the strike force was nearing its objective. The low, patchy cloud that had been predominant during the inbound flight had cleared, giving Doug perfect sight lines for their approach. Taking his position in the nose of the plane, Doug noted that the Germans were using spoof markers to try and draw the bombers away from the intended target. "Colin, the red flares to the port are clearly spoofs, and damn good ones at that," he said. "If they had been at the right height, or nearer than 25 miles from the target, I might have been fooled."

As Doug prepared to guide Colin in on the target, Colin spotted heavy flak in the area to which they were flying, the bright red flashes fading to black, the telltale smoke lingering in the air. From below came the steady stream of luminous tracers, randomly arcing through the sky like a slithering snake. For the moment at least, the intensity of the ground fire meant that flight crews need not focus on the possibility of fighters in the vicinity. Somewhat strangely, as they continued on to their objective, the searchlights stayed off.

From his prone position at the front of the plane, Doug was unaware of the churning skies around the plane as he was now completely preoccupied with making course corrections and relaying the information to Colin. As they neared the target zone, Colin reacted to the considerable flak that was being thrown up on the starboard side of the plane and immediately altered course to avoid it.

Almost instantly, a deep baritone voice thundered from below. "No. No! Stay the course! If you don't stay on the right heading, we'll miss the target!" Doug knew that his was the final word on matters respecting navigation and waited for Colin to adjust accordingly. Rather than engage in a debate at such a critical moment, Colin opted to tilt the nose of the plane slightly up, thereby affording Doug with a perfect view of what lay ahead.

"Weave! Weave!" came the cry from the navigator.

By the end of December, the Allied armies had blunted the German offensive in the Ardennes and were once again moving towards the German borders.

For Colin and Doug, six more missions had been completed, bringing their operational total to 35 since joining the squadron in September. For the squadron as a whole,

December had seen only 189 planes dispatched, with the loss of only one aircraft to a fighter. Sadly, the aircrew had also been lost.

Chapter 9

January 1945 – On the Radio

Hanau – January 1st

The new year dawned much like the previous year had ended. On December 16, 1944, the German army had launched a massive offensive in the Ardennes that was designed to split the English and American forces, forcing a halt to their relentless advance towards Germany, with the final goal being a drive to capture Antwerp. Attacking from the densely forested, snow-capped Ardennes region, the German offensive advanced rapidly against the surprised American troops. The desperate Germans pushed the Americans back across the front, eventually encircling the U.S. First Army at Bastogne.

From the outset of the operation, the Allies' air supremacy had been nullified by poor visibility. The resulting lack of air support for the embattled U.S. troops provided the Nazis with an early tactical advantage which they exploited to the fullest extent, driving the Americans back in some instances over 60 miles. As the month progressed, however, the weather system changed. The Allied forces that had stubbornly dug in and continued to defend the region against the German onslaught welcomed the appearance of Allied aircraft.

On this day, Colin and Doug and five other crews were assigned to attack Hanau, a large town some 200 miles east of the Bulge. Hanau was an important strategic target in that it represented a large transportation corridor leading from Germany to the Ardennes. The weather, having been very bad for over a week, had grounded the heavy bombers. In response, Mosquitoes were sent out to attack four separate targets. In the pre-briefing, aircrews had been instructed to vary the timing of the fuses on their bombs as a means of maximizing the effect of the attack. Unlike the usual raids where the bombs exploded shortly after striking the ground, on this mission the object was to inundate the target with explosives that might detonate over a range of times, beginning with those that would ignite instantaneously to others with delays of up to 24 hours. In so doing, the hoped-for end result was the disruption of the movement of German forces for as long as possible.

The flight crews boarded the truck for the short ride to their aircraft. The six Mosquitoes appeared like sentinels standing at a gate, silently standing guard over a small piece of rural England. The sleek lines of the planes and the absence of guns giving the appearance of a fine-tuned racing machine, rather than the lethal weapon it truly was. As the truck bounced its way to its destination, the glow from the winter sun highlighted the beauty of de Havilland's design. The tapered, light-weight frame that flashed across the skies, driven through the air by the powerful Merlin engines, and the clear sight lines that afforded the crew almost completely unobstructed views of the sky above, below, in front and behind the aircraft. As they leapt from the truck, each man felt confident in the capabilities of their plan, knowing its reputation for withstanding punishment was well earned.

Taking off at 16:30, the six aircraft arrived over the target two hours later, greeted only by slight heavy flak and the now ubiquitous spoof markers. Unlike most of the action that Colin and Doug had previously participated in, today marked one of the few times where their raid was directly in support of the ground forces engaged with the Germans. Rather than focussing on industrial facilities, the Mosquitoes raced in and distributed their payloads over main transportation routes. While success in their usual strikes would be measured by evidence of burning and wrecked factories, the returning aircrews would never know whether their efforts in Hanau achieved the desired results of disrupting German movement.

Berlin – January 14th

The 28 men listened attentively as the Wing Commander laid out the details for the operation scheduled for later that day. On the chalkboard was the now too familiar drawing of

Berlin, complete with an estimate of the defensive effort that could be expected from the Germans.

"You will be forming up with 28 other Mossies from No. 8 group to attack Berlin. Your mission is to draw attention away from a larger assault of 587 aircraft from four groups; Nos. 1, 5, 6 and 8, on the Leuna and Marseberg synthetic oil plants, some 125 miles southwest of your target. You lads will lead the first wave into Berlin, with a second wave of 42 aircraft to follow shortly thereafter. Considerable efforts will be made to confuse the enemy. In addition to your feint at Berlin, other smaller sorties will be flown against Mannheim. To supplement this activity, some of you will also be dropping Window over the Ruhr to confuse ground tracking. In addition, 100 Group will be employing a Mandrel Screen to further disrupt German signals." Pausing to survey the room, Alabaster was buoyed by the attentiveness of his men and the feeling of confidence they exuded.

"You will be flying in over Cologne and Kessel tonight, with the return leg bringing you out past Magdeburg and Hannover. For most of you, this is not your first dance over Berlin, so you know that the chances of a warm reception are very good." He smiled as he watched heads nodding and heard the mumbled epithets and curses.

"Good hunting, gentlemen."

Colin and Doug rose from their chairs and approached the blackboard to confirm what they had heard. "Not ideal weather-wise tonight," said Doug as he pored over the latest reports.

"If it's poor visibility for us, then it is poor visibility for them as well," responded Colin. "Maybe they will be smarter than us and stay on the ground."

"Yeah ... and maybe they'll surrender too," quipped the big Canadian with a slight smile.

After confirming the signals for the evening and the payload they would be carrying, the two men separated to spend a few hours preparing. As had become the recent norm, Doug set out to find a friendly game of bridge to keep his mind sharp while taking his focus off his responsibilities for that evening. Colin opted for some time by the fireplace with a cup of tea and some boisterous conversation with fellow pilots.

Later in the afternoon, the two men reconvened to take their plane through its brief test flight. Having detected no issues, upon landing, the sprightly Brit and his stoic Canuck sidekick set off for the ubiquitous pre-flight meal of bacon and eggs.

Three hours later, crammed into Mosquito KB 436 as it hurtled towards Berlin, the two men scanned the skies for signs of aircraft through the widespread mist. Having taken off after the heavy bombers, the Mosquitoes had to fly through the formation of Lancasters before turning towards Berlin with the intent of drawing the Luftwaffe away from the main body of planes.

"Did you know that there are no canaries in the Canary Islands?" joked Colin.

"What?"

"Funny thing is … that it's the same with the Virgin Islands," the smirking Brit continued. "No canaries there either!" He burst into a belly laugh.

"Stick to flying," replied Doug, doing his best to suppress a broad grin.

In the distance, the sky was now filled with hundreds of the hulking Lancasters. The Mosquito crews were fully alert to the dangers of flying through the slipstreams of the bigger aircraft as they manoeuvred around to take their place at the head of the phalanx. It was not uncommon for planes to collide in situations like this, so complete attention was required.

"Two on the port side, one at eight o'clock and one at eleven," stated Doug, pointing at the large silhouettes looming ahead of them.

"Got them, shifting course two degrees to starboard," replied the fully focussed pilot, no longer laughing, as he gently turned his plane away from harm.

Within minutes they had carved their way through the friendly formation and had reached the point to alter course. Once past the Lancasters, Doug had been studiously mapping their location in comparison to the turning point. "Time to change course to the new heading," he called out. Colin nodded and banked the plane to starboard, beginning the deeper run into Germany.

"Keep an eye out for our German friends, Doug. Here's hoping the misty skies are not to their liking."

As the attacking Mosquitoes bore down on the target, Doug began the process of climbing into position in the nose of the plane for the run in. "Show time!" he called out. While the attackers had clearly not surprised the Germans, the bad weather certainly reduced the level of response from the gun crews. Sporadic flashes could be seen in the clouds ahead, but not at the usual level of effort that the two men had come to expect when flying over Berlin. "Stay the course, Colin," he said, while scanning the skies for the target indicators.

"There … straight on … yellow target flares are drifting down!"

"Left … steady … left … steady!", guided Doug as the plane roared over Berlin.

"Bomb doors are open, Doug. It's all yours!"

"Steady … steady … on my mark … bombs are gone!" The Mosquito rose as the ton of explosives fell away into the night.

"Confirming bombs are gone! Closing bomb doors!" shouted Colin as the symphony of noise from rushing wind and bursts of flak filled the cockpit.

The wooden bomber sliced through the airstream and slowly banked away from the target.

"I can see flashes below. Must be some cookies hitting home!" called out Doug calmly. "Let's hope this was a successful diversion."

The weather conditions had indeed worked in the RAF's favour, with cloud and mist over German airfields limiting their intervention. While this had made the run in far easier, each returning aircrew now was faced with navigating their way home through less than perfect conditions. As they neared the English coast, word came through that Downham Market was not available.

"K for Kilo, this is DO. Please be advised that you are to divert to Wyton." Having noted the new coordinates, Doug quickly adjusted their heading to bring them to the new landing spot, some 30 miles southwest of Downham Market.

Not long after, Colin guided twin-engine bomber safely down, bounced across the field and taxied to a stop at the designated assembly point. As they climbed out, they were greeted by fellow 608 Squadron crewmen F/L Henderson and W/O Foley, who had also made their way south.

Target Indicator over Berlin during a Mosquito raid.

"Good to be on the ground," said Colin. "Anyone tried the chow here yet?"

The next morning, they made the short return flight to Downham Market, where they learned that the bad weather had claimed a heavy toll. Of the 83 Mosquitoes engaged in the two phases of the attack on Berlin, only 69 actually made it to the target, the rest having to abort. More importantly, eight aircraft had failed to return, two crashing over Europe and six more going down over England. Miraculously, none of the affected planes were from 608 Squadron, but the losses were felt as if they had been.

Kassel – January 21st

The plane took off just after dusk, Colin banking the plane to join the rest of the 11-plane formation as they set out to bomb factories near Kassel, Germany.

Mosquitoes were equipped with communication equipment that facilitated conversations between the pilot and the control tower as well as with the navigator. To save time, the microphones could be locked into the "world guard" or open position so that all three could converse during take-offs and landings. Having signed off with the Downham Market tower, Colin unlocked the mic and turned his attention to getting the plane to Kassel.

Crossing over the Channel, the coast of France appeared in the distance. As the French countryside passed below them, the skies remained quiet. Even the warning light panel remained silent, the red and white bulbs as dark as the enveloping sky. The mesmerizing spell was soon broken as both Colin and Doug heard voices over their intercom.

"Are you hearing this?" queried Doug, having opened his mic.

"I am. Glad to know that I am not hallucinating. I thought my oxygen might have cut out again."

As they flew, they realized they were eavesdropping on a conversation between one of the other aircrews who had inadvertently locked their microphone on "world guard". Rather than just small talk between mates, the squadron, and indeed all of Europe were now being treated to a live radio broadcast.

"Do they not realize what they are doing?" chided Colin, becoming increasingly agitated by the breach in protocol. "It's bad enough that we now all know that he's having problems at home, but anyone on the ground with an inch of common sense will now know that we are up here."

Given that radio silence was to be maintained during missions, the unplanned broadcast of the life and times of an unknown bomber crew exponentially increased the danger for the eleven planes winging their way into Germany. Gone was any chance of surprise. "Good God, we might as well be coming in with a band playing and bright lights flashing," grumbled the pilot. "This job is hard enough without giving the Nazis a heads up."

As they continued on, the situation became even graver as the anonymous crew's chatter turned to pertinent information on the mission, including details clearly indicating to all those who might be listening that they were on their way to Kassel with the intention of bombing from 25,000 feet. If that wasn't damning enough, the unknown crew even mentioned the expected time of arrival, the number of planes involved and the colour of target indicators that would be used to mark the area.

These tidbits of information drove the usually affable Brit pilot's level of consternation through the roof of the plane, as in his view, the evening's sortie had been completely compromised. "Goddamn it, Doug, the entire German air force will be dancing above Kassel waiting for us to walk into their trap!"

Stunningly, as the flight closed to within ten miles of the target, there was no evidence of any enemy activity. The fighter radar light stayed dark, and the ground radar burned only a dull red – the attack was not being followed by the radar-controlled searchlights or guns.

Ten minutes later, having dropped their payload on the intended target, the Mosquitoes turned and sped home, the confused flight crews relieved to find that the German response to the attack was minimal. In fact, the guns had only started firing well after the raid was underway.

"Bloody fools could have got us all killed," raged Colin, still angered by the sheer stupidity of the situation.

"What's the point of all the meticulous planning and security if some stupid bugger is going to announce it all to the world. A court martial would be too good for them!"

The tirade continued at the post-flight briefing, where both men made clear their views on the earlier events. The Intelligence Officer attempted to deflate the anger by pointing out that, in the end, the Germans thought it was a spoof raid and did not pay attention to the broadcast until it was too late. "Who could blame them really. The people that monitor radio waves would surely have treated this as some kind of ridiculous attempt to disguise the true purpose of our actions." And with that, the case was closed, never to be raised again. Seventy-five years later, Colin still wonders why nothing more was done.

Berlin – January 28th

Following several days of very poor weather, Colin and Doug found themselves part of a raid over Berlin being conducted by 83 Mosquitoes. After five months of duty, Doug now had considerable experience in flying in all kinds of weather and took great pride in his ability to understand the nuances required to account for changing weather patterns in order to arrive at the target area precisely on time. In particular, Doug had become quite adept at calculating the precise time to release the target indicators to ensure they were in the appropriate location for the following aircraft. He knew, for example, that in situations where the cloud cover reached 4,000 feet, the marker flares would be set with fuses that ignited via a pressure fuse at 6,000 feet and then would drift on a parachute into the clouds. If they dropped at 1,000 feet per minute, and the winds were 100 miles per hour, then in the two minutes they remained in view, the marker would have moved at least 3 miles down wind. Attention to such minute details was critical to the success of missions.

The flight into Berlin presented a new challenge for Doug and his fellow navigators; as they did their calculations to determine their positions, they discovered that the tail winds were in the order of 225 miles per hour. Not only did this mean that the determination of when to drop the target indicators had to be recalibrated, it also meant that the Mosquitoes would arrive over the target thirty minutes too soon. If the Pathfinders marked the target too early, the heavy bombers would arrive after the flares had burned out and would be bombing blind. Making the mathematics even more complicated was the fact that the heavy bombers were flying 5,000 feet lower than the Mosquitoes, where the winds were not as strong.

Doug altered the flight plan to account for all the variables and relayed the changes to Colin. "We need to swing out to the east and then turn back into the wind before beginning our run in on the target." After a few minutes of flying into the strong winds, Doug called to Colin to bring the plane back into the jet stream and steer for the target zone.

While all of this was happening, the Germans were preparing to welcome the intruders with as heavy a barrage as was possible. The extra time afforded by the adjustments needed to align the Pathfinders with the heavy bombers afforded the defenders additional time to maximize their efforts. What the Germans could not allot for was the impact of the winds on the speed of the attacking aircraft. When Colin and Doug make their bombing run, their ground speed was 625 miles per hour, some 200 miles per hour more than usual. The exaggerated speed meant that, as a result, the anti-aircraft gunners, firing at planes that they expected were flying at their usual rate of speed, were shooting the sky full of holes about a mile or so behind the attacking aircraft.

The clear skies over the target afforded the bombers an unrestricted view of the results of their efforts. As the Mosquitoes roared over the city, the sky was alight with a 16-mile-long trail of target indicators running north to south across the entire target area. As they turned to leave, Colin and Doug could see the telltale explosions of the 4,000-pound bombs of the bigger planes as they rained down on the built-up area of Berlin, the ground seemingly rolling under the massive concussions.

Having completed their mission, the aircrews were now faced with flying into same winds that had benefited their attack. Once again, the aviation gods exacted a heavy toll for what had been a beneficial flight in by forcing the returning planes to extricate themselves from German airspace at a greatly reduced speed. As they flew towards the German borders, the clear skies over Berlin were replaced by heavy, low cloud with poor visibility. As the planes cleared the continent and winged their way over the water, fuel issues began to plague many of the aircraft. As a result of the severe atmospheric conditions, eight of the original eighty-three Mosquitoes crashed, five going down in England and three in Belgium, the heaviest loss of the wooden bombers in a single night of the war.

Colin and Doug fared better than most, arriving over England with sufficient fuel. Unfortunately, they were soon informed that it was not going to be an easy final route in.

"K as in Kilo, you are advised to reroute to Wyton. DO is obscured by fog and low-lying cloud and is inoperable."

"Right-o," exclaimed Colin. "How are we doing for fuel, Doug?"

"We are good to go" he replied as he quickly plotted their location and directed Colin to alter course to Wyton. Some four hours and fifteen minutes after leaving Downham Market, flying into the steady headwinds on the return to England, the pair had made the round trip to Berlin in 45 fewer minutes than had been their previous experience. Such had been the effect of the tail winds on the outbound leg of the journey.

Upon debriefing, the two men were informed that they had experienced what was known as the Japanese Jet Stream, a condition commonly experienced by the Allies in the Pacific as they flew through the strong winds near Japan.

As January closed, a month dogged by poor weather, the two men had added another seven sorties to their resumé, bringing their total to 41. The squadron had managed only 120 sorties over the course of the month. Incredibly, by the 31st, the group had been largely unscathed, with only one aircraft damaged.

On the ground, the war continued to grind along. The German offensive in the Ardennes had been checked and reversed, with Allied forces continuing their push towards Germany.

Ian Redmond

Chapter 10

February 1945 - Snappers

Erfurt – February 19th

After four nights of cancellations due to inclement weather, seventeen Mosquitoes took to the air on this night to strike at oil-related targets near Erfurt, a large city 186 miles southwest of Berlin. The squadron had successfully pressed home the attack, with Colin and Doug dropping their four 500-pound bombs from only 12,000 feet.

The flight in and the bombing run had been uneventful for a change, with little flak thrown their way and the absence of any night fighters. "One could get used to that," mused Colin, thinking to himself he should probably not have spoken too soon. And, as one could expect when dealing with the flying gods, the ideal mission did take a sudden change. As the returning planes neared England, the weather took a nasty turn. The relatively light clouds and clear visibility that had marked the air column over Europe were replaced with a blanket of thick, impenetrable clouds and fog that covered Downham Market.

As they passed the coast, their headsets came alive. "All flights, be advised that FIDO is operational and landings will proceed accordingly," came the instructions. For Colin and Doug, this would be their first experience with landing using the Fog Investigation and Dispersal Operation (FIDO) system. Originally conceived by Winston Churchill, FIDO consisted of two pipelines situated along both sides of the runway. Fuel, usually the petrol from the airfield's own fuel dump, was pumped along and then out through burner jets positioned at intervals along the pipelines. The vapours were lit from a series of burners, producing walls of flame. The concept was simple; the heat from the flames would disperse dense clouds and fog around the airfield so that incoming aircraft could land safely.

While still a hundred miles out from home, Colin and Doug were able to discern a glow on the horizon that marked their destination. Even so, the glow could only give the pair a general sense of where they were headed. Getting them precisely on point was going to take all of Doug's considerable navigation skills, particularly since there were no stars visible to assist with the calculations.

"I know where we were when we entered this pea soup," Doug pointed out in his usual calm manner. "Give me a second to run that against the prevailing winds and our air speed. Should be able to give you a good idea of where we are."

Colin had learned over time that his partner was incredibly precise in his computations. In point of fact, his pronouncements had an almost gospel-like quality, as they unerringly brought them over targets hundreds of miles from England precisely on time and on location. He had no reason to doubt that this same skill set would deliver them precisely to Downham Market, particularly with the added benefit of a glow guiding them in.

That being said, however, Colin could not shake the thought that flying blind as they descended would certainly bring other variables into play, most notably the changing topography or the existence of such things as church spires or radar towers. Taking care not to deflate his friend's ego, Colin turned to him and politely asked, "You don't mind if I go up a few thousand feet and swing out over the ocean, just to be sure, do you?"

Doug turned to him, with a slight smile on his face, nodded and said, "Sure ... beats running into a hillside." After five months together, the two men clearly thought as one.

Colin adjusted the flight path and prepared for the final approach. Soon after, the call came in. "R as in Roger, you are next to land."

The glow through the clouds was quite pronounced as they approached the airfield, with the heat-induced clouds swirling above the runway lit up like a patio lantern. Colin dropped the plane lower, turning towards the now visible line of burning petrol that paralleled the landing strip. As they descended through the remaining ice and fog, each man became aware of a sudden burst of light as they passed over the stream of flames at the end of the runway, followed by entry into what seemed like a tunnel of intense flames leading them home.

Mosquito landing under FIDO
(Source: Aircrew Remembered)

The Mosquito bounced its way across the runway, careening towards the wall of fire that marked the end of the tarmac. One more prodigious bounce pushed the pair past the FIDO flames, after which the plane disappeared into the gloom at the end of the field. "Home again," exclaimed Colin.

"Nice work," came the reply.

As the two men exited their plane, they found themselves parked about 20 feet short of the control tower. No need to wait for a ride in," said Doug, as they strolled towards the building to give their mandatory debriefing.

Berlin – February 22nd

Three nights after their indoctrination with the intricacies of landing in the thick English fog, Colin and Doug found themselves flying to Berlin for the second consecutive night. Berlin continued to be the crown jewel of targets for Bomber Command. Bomber Harris still clung to his belief that battering the Third Reich's capital city would lead the Nazi leadership to the inevitable conclusion that the war was lost. "I understand the thinking behind this," said Doug as they made their way in to the target. "I just wish someone would tell the buggers manning the searchlights and guns that their fight is futile."

"You'll get no argument from me," replied the diminutive pilot, flashing his ever-present smile.

As the twelve Mosquitoes closed in on their target, the electronics on each of the aircraft were getting a thorough workout. German ground tracking devices and homing-in radar in the noses of their fighters operated on different frequencies. To assist aircrew in combatting the different German defence systems, Mosquitoes were equipped with a short antenna, about 15 inches long, that extended from the tail end of the fuselage. Know as "boozer", it was capable of picking up incoming signals from these detection devices and separating them based on their frequencies. In the cockpit of the plane, a small instrument was fitted near where one might find the rear-view mirror on a car. Attached to this instrument were two lights. When a ground station was tracking the plane, the light showed a dull red. When the tracking was turned over to the searchlight radar, the light changed to bright red. When this happened, it meant the pilot and navigator could expect to be coned by searchlights at any moment, unless violent evasive action was taken. Dull red was not particularly alarming as it merely meant that the entire flight of aircraft was being tracked. The change to bright red meant that your plane had been singled out for a bath of bright lights, complete with the resulting increase in anxiety.

More problematic for the Mosquito crew was the sudden appearance of a white light, the signal that tracking had been turned over to a fighter and that the Mosquito was on a German pilot's radar. If the fighter made visual contact, the game changed considerably. When a fighter could see a Mosquito, it could move in for the kill. A white light meant evasive manoeuvres, sometimes violent ones, were imperative immediately. The only time when an aircrew might ignore a sudden white light was during the run in to drop the bomb load. In such instances, an aircrew had been schooled that they must continue straight and level until the target markets and explosives were dropped on the target.

On this particular night, the warning lights were given an exhaustive test, as the ground station radar system picked up the squadron from the moment it crossed into Germany. The dull red light glared at Colin and Doug like moonlight reflecting the eyes of a rabid animal watching them from the darkness. But as they entered the phalanx of searchlights west of the capital city, the light went to a bright red.

If that was not sufficiently harrowing, on the flight in, most of the planes in their group had experienced, at one time or another, the indication that a fighter was on their tail. At this late juncture of the war, this was of particular concern given the arrival of jet fighters into the German's air defence arsenal. The Messerschmitt 262 represented a significantly more deadly adversary than the Messerschmitt BF 109G or the Focke Wulf 190, the workhorses of the German fighter arm. Unlike the BF 198G with its 2 machine guns and 3 cannons, and the FW190's 2 machine guns and 4 cannons, the jet carried four cannons and 24 rockets. The difference in fire power was markedly higher. Where a three-second burst from the BF 109G would fire 35 pounds of ammunition and a FW 190 would expend 37 pounds of ordinance, a ME 262 expended 96 pounds (not including the striking power of the rockets).

Unlike other German fighters that were easily outpaced by the Mosquito, the ME 262 could fly at speeds that exceeded the Mosquito's top range by 100 mph. This represented a significant disadvantage for the wooden bombers. Not only were the fighters faster, they were also equipped with their own radar system to allow them to home in on Allied aircraft. Used as a night fighter, the jets shot down 13 Mosquitoes over Berlin in the first three months of 1945, a significant increase in fatalities from the previous 12 months.

RAF pilots quickly learned that the Mosquito still had an important tactical advantage over the new technology; the wooden wonder could outmaneuver the ME 262 at maximum height and speed as the bomber could execute a 180 degree turn within a 4-mile diameter circle. The ME 262 required 8 miles to do the same. Experience also taught aircrews that the new jet was limited to about 45 to 60 minutes of flying time, which, combined with its need for an exceptionally long runway for takeoff, meant that they did not fly too far from their home base. If one could elude the menacing jet for 20 minutes, there was a good chance that it would turn away to head for home. RAF intelligence reports also found that while a ME 262 could land on a smaller runway, its inability to take off from such facilities meant that the planes had to be dismantled and returned to their home airfield by rail before they could be reassembled and flown again. This was a particularly serious issue for the Luftwaffe, given that the combined Allied Air Forces were pounding German rail facilities and strafing any trains that might venture out during the daylight hours.

In response to the potential threat created by the new German weapon, Colin and Doug had an agreement that should either of them notice the white light come on, they would yell, "White light!" and Colin would immediately dive the plane to a lower height and change their heading. If the light ignited and there was clear evidence of a jet in the vicinity, regular squadron protocol could be broken as aircrew had been given the okay to break radio silence, calling out "snappers" to quickly alert the bombing force to the potential threat. Each plane would then take evasive action, knowing that the key to survival was avoiding the jet making visual contact with the bomber.

Having just completed their bomb run, Colin turned the plane for home. Within seconds, Colin called out, "White light!" Without hesitation, he powered the bomber into a steep dive down to 10,000 feet.

"What are you doing?" exclaimed Doug.

"The light is on. I am not waiting until it is too late to take action!" came the authoritative reply. "Snappers! Snappers!" Colin called out as he leveled the Mosquito out at its new height. Still the light continued to blaze. "Hang on, Doug, the bugger is still looking for us!" he yelled as he pushed the plane to starboard, while at the same time climbing again. Colin continued to fly like the plane was bobbing on the surf near some summer ocean resort. And still the light stayed on.

"I can't see him!" yelled Doug, as he twisted in his seat, scanning the skies to their rear.

"If you could see him, we'd be dead," came the response.

After corkscrewing and weaving across the sky for over 30 minutes, the light went out. The two men breathed a collective sigh. "Persistent little shit," mumbled Colin. "He must have given up and returned to base."

"Do you think that it might have only been atmospheric interference?" queried Doug.

"Would you rather I had taken the chance to find out?"

"Hmmm, no."

The rest of the flight home was uneventful, although the dull red light remained their companion until they passed out of Germany and flew over open waters. On return, each of the aircrew reported this intense activity by the enemy to Intelligence, except for Flight Lieutenant Ford and Flying Officer Hebden, who reported the quietest trip ever to Berlin. Ford reported having seen a dull red warning light for only a short interval shortly after entering Germany, when it shone only for an instant, then went out. The white light had stayed dark.

It was only later that night that Ford and Hebden learned that the aerial had been shot off their plane. Ignorance was bliss.

Berlin – February 23rd

Word spread quickly across the base. Twelve aircraft had been sent over Berlin as a feint attack to draw attention away from the heavy bombers that targeted Pferzheim and the U-boat pens at Herten. As dawn approached, only 11 had safely returned. Mosquito "B for Bravo" had not been heard from since take-off.

In the briefing room, those in charge of monitoring the missions had chalked in the dreaded "missing" notation in the column beside plane B. The loss of a plane could be overcome, but the loss of an aircrew was a devastating blow to the squadron. For the men that flew the Mosquitoes, it was a harsh reality check; they were not invincible. As a particularly tight group, with bonds forged over the deadly skies over Germany, the loss of colleagues affected the group as a whole.

As the day progressed, each man clung to the faint hope that the missing plane had found its way safely to another base or that the crew had safely parachuted from their stricken aircraft. While they awaited news, the business of the airfield continued unchecked. Preparations were underway for the next sortie. Crews were selected; briefings were prepared; aircraft were serviced and armed; and, personnel tended to their responsibilities. By late morning, confirmation had been received; the missing plane had gone down over Germany. F/L Robert Doherty and F/O Leonard Moore had paid the ultimate price.

Death was no stranger to Bomber Command. For those who had known the grief of losing comrades, the advice to others was always the same. Don't dwell on it, just press on. Press on. Bury the anguish deep within oneself and get on with the job. Don't talk about what might have happened, just focus on the next mission.

Easily said, but whenever someone glanced at the empty cot in the Nissen hut or the locker in the crew assembly area, thoughts immediately turned to the men who had occupied that space the night before. The grim reality finally settled in when someone was sent to gather up their things and put them in kit bags. This was not unique to the air war; soldiers, sailors and civilians alike had suffered losses and known the emptiness of death, the hollowed-out spot in the soul and the search for the answer to why. Over time, each man and woman would find the way to cope, whether sharing stories and a pint at the pub, seeking strength from their beliefs or putting all of their energy into doing their job as best they could. For many of the survivors, the time for grieving came well after the war had ended … if it came at all.

Neuss – February 24th

Two nights after the white light festival, Colin and Doug were once again tasked with striking into Germany, this time making their way to Neuss, a small city in the Rhine region near Dusseldorf. As they crossed into Germany, a red streak appeared ahead that was rising fast and changing colour as it rose. Instantly, Colin and several other pilots broke radio silence with the "snappers" call.

"Hold on, Colin. That isn't right!" said Doug. Having watched the path of the streak, Doug had noted that it was nearly vertical. "See the colour changes – that tells me whatever it is, it is flying through changing levels of atmospheric pressure. You don't see that with a fighter."

"Bloody hell, man, that is clearly a jet," responded Colin icily, feeling unnecessarily chastised for having done what he felt was clearly the correct thing.

Doug too was feeling a bit put off that his analysis was not being given proper consideration. "It is not a jet," he stated flatly. "The trail of the flight is not horizontal, it's vertical."

"What do you mean vertical? It's clearly flying across our horizon," retorted Colin.

"It only appears that way because we are now flying on our left side," stated Doug, pointing at the instrument panel. Indeed, Colin had been so intent on following the trail of the unknown object, he had lost track of the horizon and had turned the plane on its side. Quickly righting the aircraft, it became apparent that the object had indeed flown high over them.

"My God," muttered Colin. "What was that?"

It was only upon their return to Downham Market that they learned that this had been their first sighting of a V2, a forty-six-foot-long rocket with a warhead that contained nearly a ton of explosives. One of the German wonder weapons, the rocket was seen as a means to wreak havoc on England in hopes of changing the tide of the war. Difficult to defend against once launched given their excessive speed, the Allies were at a loss to develop counter measures that would destroy them in flight. Instead, attempts were made to watch them once launched with the object being to provide warning, if indeed that was possible since the time between launch and detonation over England was very short.

Recognizing the futility of that approach, attention focussed on identifying the launching points and annihilating them through bombing. Allied High Command soon determined that in addition to destroying launch sites, the bombing of bridges in the vicinity of the launch pads would cut the German's ability to supply rockets to them, thereby reducing the risk.

For Colin and Doug, the first encounter was not the last. In fact, Doug would later note that on a clear night, one could time the length of the rocket's flight from takeoff to the appearance of a bright flash in England some eight minutes later.

Erfurt – February 25th

For the second time in a week, Colin and Doug were to be part of a 15-plane attack on the oil facilities in Erfurt. At 18:30, KB 406 lifted into the air. The base meteorologist had briefed the crews to expect relatively clear skies over the target, similar to the weather system that the planes encountered as they made their way across the English Channel.

As they flew over France, Colin and Doug were still buzzing about their encounter with the V2 on the previous evening.

"Don't you find it disconcerting that German technology continues to advance at such a tremendous rate?" asked Doug. "We seem to be crossing paths with more rocket-based weaponry every week."

"I thought that the jet fighters were frightening enough. But what we saw last night is something entirely different," responded Colin, pausing briefly before continuing. "It makes what we're doing doubly important, old man. The only way to stop these weapons is to destroy them on the ground. Once they are in the air, people will be relying on the good graces of whatever god they pray to."

Suddenly, the Mosquito shook and wobbled. "What the hell?" exclaimed Colin. "We have a problem!" Glancing to his left, he could see the port propeller slowing down. A quick check of instruments confirmed that the engine had failed. The two men were now cruising in a fully laden bomber that was running on a single engine.

Colin switched on his microphone, alerting Downham Market of the situation and seeking permission to return. "Understood, K as in King, you are cleared to abort," came the rapid response.

Colin examined the starboard engine and made a quick decision. "DO, we cannot make it to you. Need alternative landing site." The men were quickly instructed to make their way to Woodbridge, a US air base on the English coast, near Ipswich. Without hesitation, Doug computed the coordinates and Colin gently turned the plane to limp back to England.

"We can't bring her home with a full bomb load," said Doug. "We need to jettison them now." Colin quickly agreed. As Doug swung down to his bomb-aimer position, the bomb bay doors opened. Still over the channel, Doug peered down to ensure that there were no vessels below. The clear skies afforded a decent view, the moonlight shimmering off the water below. After a quick look, it was determined that the seas were clear. Doug pressed the trigger and the four bombs dropped away. The loss of the ton of explosives dramatically reduced the weight of the aircraft, making flight to Woodbridge marginally easier.

Thankfully the Mosquito was quite capable of maintaining flight with one engine feathered. As they flew, Colin was reminded of a line he had heard months before from a Lancaster pilot. "You know, Doug, some have said that the only reason to have two engines is that when one fails, the good one can take you to the scene of the crash," he said with a smile. The grim glance he received in response quickly wiped it off his face.

Twenty minutes later, cleared to land by the Woodbridge tower, the Mosquito gently touched down and taxied off the runway, lost amidst the larger four-engine behemoths lining the airfield.

Having safely landed, and with their plane in need of considerable work, they decided to take advantage of the situation and visit the officers mess for a meal. It was well known in RAF circles that the food available to the Americans at their airfields was far superior to that provided to the RAF crews. Without hesitation, the two men helped themselves to steak and eggs and proceeded to find a table to enjoy this unexpected feast.

They had barely sat down when a Warrant Officer approached the table. "Excuse me, sirs. I've been asked to tell you that there is a pilot waiting to ferry you back to your home base."

"Thank you, lad," responded Colin. "Would you please inform the pilot that we are going to enjoy our meal first. I am sure he can wait a few minutes."

The young officer saluted and turned away. "Well, then, where were we," said Colin, as he cut into the healthy sized steak.

"Colin," interrupted Doug, "we have company." Looking up, Colin watched as the young Warrant Officer crossed the room, heading directly for them.

"Excuse me again, sirs," he began sheepishly, "the pilot was extremely agitated with the response and asked that I make it clear that you are expected to make your way to his plane immediately."

"I don't care if it is the Wing Commander himself, we are eating first," replied Colin, somewhat tersely.

When they eventually made their way to the dispersal area, they were indeed met by a visibly upset WC Alabaster.

Giving the two men a withering stare, he admonished them. "If you had gotten back to me when I first called for you, we would have made it back to the field in time for you to pick up a spare plane and join the raid. Now our squadron's perfect record is in jeopardy!"

While outwardly appearing to feel shame, Colin snuck a sly glance at Doug. As the Wing Commander boarded the plane, Colin whispered to Doug that he really wasn't very sorry to have missed it, preferring a fine meal instead.

The tide of the war was now decidedly with the Allies. The leaders of the three Allied powers, Great Britain, the United States and Russia, had met in Yalta to discuss the final phase of the war, including the occupation of Germany.

By the end of February, Colin and Doug had completed 48 sorties totalling 391.5 hours over Germany. During the same time period, the squadron completed 236 sorties, with the loss of two aircraft.

Ian Redmond

Chapter 11

March 1945 – Last Dance

Berlin – March 1st

On this night, Colin and Doug carried three 500 lb bombs and one target indicator. As Pathfinders, their role was to mark the target for the following main force of bombers. It was nights like this that weighed heavily on the shoulders of Doug and his fellow Pathfinder navigators. Bomber Command asked nothing more of its personnel than to be reliable, meaning in the navigators' context that they be accurate in their course plotting and precise in the timing of the target marking. Bent over his charts and logs, armed with his pencils and instruments as always, Doug concentrated his entire being on the task at hand, pushing out any negative thoughts and suppressing any anxiety about what even the slightest error might mean for the aircrews to follow and the objectives of the operation. He knew that arriving over the target for the initial marking had to be on time. A few minutes on either side could mean the difference between success and survival, or disaster.

It was for this reason that Bomber Command sought out the best aircrews to man their Pathfinder squadrons. The skills and abilities of the pilots and navigators, men like Colin and Doug, were so well honed that they could arrive over a target within 30 seconds of the planned time after several hours and hundreds of miles of flying. Quite simply, aircrews were required to exercise intensive effort to regularly find their position and, as necessary, adjust and amend their course to bring them to the identified point at the allotted time.

On this night, the raid on Berlin was intended to check the effectiveness of the Long-Range Navigation (LORAN) system that had been used for some time as a navigational aid over the North Atlantic. In 1944, two control stations were established, one near Edinburgh and a second near Bengazi. The signals from these two sites could provide quite effective coverage of Europe east of the Rhine River. In order to test LORAN, the sky in the area had to be cleared of other Allied aircraft and the instrument had to be used throughout the operation. A reading was taken every six minutes and a camera mounted on a tripod over the set recorded the readings and any interference that might occur. Bombs were dropped when the readings indicated that the plane was over the target.

As sorties moved deeper into Germany, bombing using LORAN navigation had been found to be less accurate than had previously been the case. It was recognized that the Germans had become more adept at jamming the system, but even in instances where jamming was not experienced, results were worse than anticipated. Several crews, including Colin and Doug, had reported that radar beams seemed to be deflecting as they crossed the Alps. In order to test this theory, 608 Squadron was tasked with taking readings and photographs to assist with amending flight charts to correct for the expected distortion.

As was always the case when flying over Berlin, the sky was alive with light and sound; the blue-yellow beams from the searchlights were interspersed with the flashes of red and yellow from the dreaded 88mm cannons below. Colin held the plane steady as it bounced through the concussions of the explosions, ever cognizant of the speed and height of the aircraft. Below him, Doug was fixated on the bomb aiming, once again holding the release mechanism in a death grip. "Keep her steady, Colin," he called over the intercom. "We are on line, two minutes out." Two minutes. A small amount of time, yet, with what seemed to be the whole of the German anti-aircraft defenses seeking them out, it passed in what seemed like an eternity.

"Marker ready ... bombs ready," advised Doug, and at the right moment, they were released. As was the case in each and every raid, Colin flew the plane through the maelstrom, ignoring the flashes and bangs while the onboard camera whirled and clicked, recording the outcomes of their action. As they cleared the target zone, Colin banked the bomber away from the action.

"Okay Doug, time to get us the bloody hell out of here!"

Upon return to Downham Market, the exhausted crew quickly debriefed the Intelligence Officer on what they had encountered, trusting that the information contained on their film would be corroborated by reports from spies on the ground on the exact location of the bombs' impact. Instead of an assessment of the success of the evening's work, Colin and Doug were told that the photo technician had forgotten to put film in their camera, without which a proper assessment of the amended charts could not be made. "Gentlemen," he told them, "I am afraid we will have to do this all over again."

While their eyes betrayed their reaction to this news, neither man spoke. As they made their way to the Mess, it was Colin who broke the silence. "

"Do it again? Like it is just a walk in the park! All they had to do was load some film!"

"I'll check it myself next time!' chimed in Doug. "I'm sure I can find some spare time to do their job too!"

Berlin - March 3rd

The day had begun just like countless others over the past six months, the routine embedded in their subconscious: a cold shave and wash; breakfast in the Mess; and then word that they would be flying that evening. The preparatory process was now second nature to the two men. But on this day, there was a strange sense of foreboding. On forty-nine previous occasions, the pair had flown into the crucible of fire, ignoring the ever-present danger and returning home, perhaps miraculously, to fight another day. Today, the feeling was different.

Fifty missions. The end of their tour of duty. Since forming their partnership, the previous September, Colin and Doug had logged over 230 hours of flying time over Germany, dodging enemy aircraft, passing through dazzling searchlights, and bucking and thrashing their way through hails of anti-aircraft fire. Fear was a constant companion in the cold, dark skies, whispering in their ears, seeking to cause doubt and uncertainty. Would that next flash of light engulf their Mosquito? Would a night fighter slip in behind them and deliver a killing blow? Somehow, the two men had suppressed these thoughts, losing themselves in the details of flying an airplane several hundred miles, arriving at the designated target within seconds of the intended time, and delivering their payload of marker flares and explosives to clearly mark the area for the heavy bombers that followed them in.

Still, as they made their way to the afternoon briefing session, the unspoken reality was that this could be their last flight together, regardless of how events unfolded. For the first time, there was an end point within sight. Fifty sorties meant that they could stand down from active duty and move on to the next phase of their military service. As heady a thought as that might be, neither man could dwell on the possibilities that lay ahead. There still was one more mission to accomplish, and one more blow to strike against a ruthless and pitiless adversary. The single-minded focus required to achieve that evening's goals pushed out all extraneous thoughts.

Taking their place in the briefing room, they waited patiently for the base commander to arrive. Within minutes, WC Alabaster entered and quickly unveiled the designated target for that night: Berlin. Of course, it would be Berlin – the epicentre of the Third Reich – complete with its seemingly impenetrable defences. Twelve Mosquitoes would be making their way to the sprawling city, intent on inflicting significant damage on rail lines and transportation hubs. If a crew only had one more kick at the can, it might just as well be against the biggest strategic target in Germany.

Having reviewed the predicted weather and the expected German response, the briefing session adjourned. As each crew made their way out of the room, Doug paused to gaze at the mission board, noting with a strange satisfaction that they were one of the lead aircraft for the raid. He turned and made his way out of the building, joining Colin before making their way to their quarters to while away the few hours before the afternoon test flight, the pre-flight meal and gearing up. As they walked, neither man talked, preferring to keep their inner thoughts to themselves.

Later that day, as they clambered aboard KB 424, a Mosquito Mk XX, Doug tapped the fuselage and quietly muttered, "Ok, girl, you can do this."

Once in place, the pair performed the perfunctory checks, each man declaring that everything was in order. The go signal received, Colin revved the engines and released the brakes, sending the bomber hurtling down the runway. At 18:15, the plane cleared the earth, rose to join its squadron mates and banked towards Berlin.

The skies were clear on the flight in, the red light in the cockpit mildly glowing, an indication that ground radar was tracking their progress. Happily, the white light stayed unlit; at least there would be no added distraction of evading a pursuing fighter. Ten minutes out, Doug slid into his "office" to prepare for the bombing run. Almost on cue, the sky lit up with the probing beams of light that Colin and Doug had become accustomed to, followed shortly thereafter by the bright red flashes signifying the arrival of the dreaded ack-ack fire. As Colin stared ahead, he was once again greeted by the appearance of what seemed to be an impenetrable wall of fire that was directly in their path. Experience had taught him that there were, in fact, great gaps between the exploding shells once you were in the midst of them; one needed only to remain calm and stay the course.

At precisely 20:32, Doug announced that the bombs were away, seeming to perfectly bracket the red and green target indicator flares. Bright flashes appeared on the ground as the onboard camera recorded their efforts. "We're done here," stated Doug. "Take us home, Colin." Within seconds, the speedy bomber banked away from the target area, seeking out the relative safety of darkness.

As they made their way to the coast, away from the seemingly endless symphony of flashes and bangs that surrounded Berlin, the two men began to think about what they had accomplished over their time together. While neither man would consider himself to be superstitious, they still would not allow themselves to express their feelings about their time together until they were safely down and home in Downham Market.

Unbeknownst to them and the other planes that had made up the attacking force on that evening, the Germans were instituting a new tactic in the defence of their air space. As the various squadrons thundered across the sky on their way back to England, German night fighters were trailing behind them, as part of what was to known to the Luftwaffe as *Unternehmen Gisela* (Operation Gisela), the last major operation launched by the German night fighters during the war.

By this point in the war, German air defences were stressed to the breaking point. Much of their early warning capacity had been lost when the Allied armies had rolled through the previously occupied territories, which, combined with lack of experienced night fighter crews and almost crippling shortage of fuel, was making it nearly impossible to slow the Bomber Command onslaught.

In a desperate attempt to improve the situation and hamper British operations, a number of experienced night fighter commanders and pilots suggested restarting intruder operations over England, a strategy that had met with some success in 1940 and 1941. Hermann Goering, commander-in-chief of the Luftwaffe sanctioned the operation, and on this night, the Germans were poised to strike.

Colin and Doug were one of over 500 Allied aircraft involved in raids across Germany on this night. As they flew home, behind and below them came German fighters. The first Junkers 88s, armed with four 7.9 mm machine guns and individual radar, took off at 23:00 and began heading toward the Dutch coast where they dived to sea level and stayed at approximately 150 feet while they flew out to sea. Crews were forbidden to engage enemy aircraft over the North Sea in order to preserve surprise until the last possible moment. The weather over the English coast was overcast, with rain squalls helping to hide the German planes. The rain assisted the German crews in judging the location and distance above the water. Once the British coast was reached, the German planes climbed to the height of the returning bomber stream and released their version of Window to confuse the radar of the Allied fighters.

As the bombers crossed over the English coast, the first attacks occurred. The station commander at Oulton reported an intruder over his station and soon after radar screens picked up large numbers of hostile aircraft. The headquarters of 100 Group were alerted and a scramble order given to Mosquito fighter squadrons. A "scram" order was also issued to bomber units still airborne; it signified a warning to bomber crews that intruders were in the vicinity and they were to divert to airfields in western or southern England, and out of danger. Even with the warning, the Germans were able to press on their attack, firing on bombers as they approached their airfields and, in some cases, strafing the planes as they taxied on the ground.

Onboard Mosquito KB 424, the white light illuminated as the English shoreline loomed ahead. Without hesitation, Colin took evasive action. As he did so, the airwaves came alive with reports of night fighters popping up amidst the returning bombers. Any thoughts about the end of the tour of duty were quickly replaced by more immediate concerns of survival. Nearing Downham Market, Colin was relieved to hear the dulcet tones of the on-duty WAAF, guiding him in. They touched down at 22:25, quickly brought their plane to its designated spot and then scrambled away to debrief the base Intelligence Officer.

By 02:15, the attacks were over. During the course of the action, 42 bombers of various types were shot down and another 8 were badly damaged, though none of those impacted were from 608 Squadron. Over the coming days, it became clear the *Gisela* had failed to achieve the results hoped for. The Allied onslaught continued undiminished, and the German losses sustained in the operation far outweighed the successes. Unlike the seemingly endless supply of aircrew of the Allies, the Luftwaffe could no longer replace downed aircraft and pilots. The air war over Germany was rapidly coming to a close.

For Colin and Doug, it was an unexpected send-off for their term of operations. The immediacy of the final few minutes of the mission having completely turned their attention away from what they had achieved: 50 bombing missions against targets within Germany over 180 days.

As they sat through their debriefing, WC Alabaster entered the room. When he spotted the two men, he made his way towards them, with a broad smile on his face. "I've got some news for you two boys," he said. "You're screened."

It took a moment to sink in, but as it did, there was a strange rush of emotions: elation at having cheated the Grim Reaper and survived a full tour of duty; sadness for those who had not been so fortunate; and, a bittersweet realization that they would no longer be flying with the man with whom they had become so close and relied on so heavily. They saluted the Wing Commander and then shook hands. Then they turned their attention to their most pressing need ... food.

Now as they sat down for a welcome meal and a warm cup of tea, they looked around and contemplated where life would take them next. For the first time since their initial foray to Hannover six months earlier, they were now in a position to consider what their long term goals could be. No longer would they live day-to-day, suppressing their fears over the uncertainty of life as a Bomber Command aircrew. Their days of flying into the forge that was Nazi German air space was over. They basked in an incredible sense of accomplishment, before spending a brief moment of reflection for those who had been lost over that time period. True to their personalities, the pair kept their thoughts to themselves, soon parting for the night as they made their way to their respective beds. As he turned away from Colin, Doug reached into his pocket, pulled out the crushed bag of spam sandwiches and casually tossed it into a nearby trash bin for the last time.

A Last Dinner

They were now posted out. No longer part of active operations. Both men were able to contemplate where their lives might take them. For Doug, the thought of going home to be with his bride filled his day. For Colin, whose wife, Kath, had been nearby for the past few months, the idea of continuing to fly in some non-combat capacity was appealing.

On March 21st, the two men got together for one last meal before Doug was to ship out. Doug arranged to meet Colin and his wife in town at the Crown Hotel for a pleasant evening of good food and idle conversation. Of course, as could be expected, talk soon turned introspective as each man reflected on what they had experienced since the day they had fortuitously come together the previous September.

"Think about it, Doug. Fifty times we flew into Germany, never once fretting over what might happen to us," Colin began, pausing only to sip on his whiskey. "Well, perhaps once or twice."

"If you stop and think about it now, it's pretty alarming what we did," Doug added, sitting back in his chair.

"Really", continued Colin. "To go into this business thinking that nothing disastrous would ever happen to you is both unjustified and irrational."

"And yet," responded Doug, "here we are. Unscarred, feet planted firmly on the ground and able to embrace whatever tomorrow might bring."

As they sat, other personnel from the base could be seen walking through town or dining at a nearby table. "I feel somewhat ashamed to be walking away from this when there is still work to be done. When we were asked at the outset to sign up for a second tour of duty, I thought it was a ridiculous suggestion, but now I can appreciate the lure of just one more mission," said Colin.

"I think I can honestly say that I have seen enough horror and felt enough sadness to last for a lifetime. For six months, we were damned lucky, as my uniform can attest. We did everything we were ordered to do and somehow managed to get home safely. I don't feel the need to tempt the fates once more. Let's leave that to those other brave chaps that will continue the fight."

Kath looked at them both and chimed in. "I, for one, am glad to have you on the ground with me. Doug, I suspect that your wife will be equally pleased that your tour has ended and you're no longer flying in harm's way."

"You're quite right," responded Doug, "Hazel would never forgive me if I signed on again."

Doug raised his glass, gazed around the room, and uttered a brief toast. "To the end of the war."

"If I may," followed Colin. "To those who went before us and those who still fly."

Another round was ordered as dishes were cleared away.

"Do you think we made a difference?" asked Doug as he looked out at the street and the big clock that dominated the market square.

"I like to think so," came the response. "For the English, we knew we were fighting a battle for survival. I never think of it in terms of casualties. I just know that if we had lost, all was lost. You know," Colin continued, "it wasn't something that you Canadians *had* to do. You just threw in your weight gallantly behind us. You did … so did the South Africans and the Australians. They didn't have to do it, but they have all rallied round." Raising his glass again, he looked around the room and said, "To those who made a difference … thank you!"

"To the difference makers!" echoed Doug. "And thank you too".

When they parted company that evening, the two men who had been inseparable for six months, sharing moments of boredom, elation and terror, walked away, never to see each other again. Stoic to the last, they never spoke of how, for fifty missions, they had relied on each others' skills and courage to survive against the odds and to do their part to hasten the end of the war.

Ian Redmond

Chapter 12

Post Script

Douglas Redmond

Over the next five and half months, Doug found himself as the Acting Station Navigation Officer at the #22 Operational Training Unit in Wellsbourne Mountford, before posting to Bomber Command Instructors School at Finningly, where he completed an Aircrew Navigator special Category "D" instructional course with the designation of Category A2. By July, he was the chief Navigation Officer for #22.

On August 4, 1945, he was posted to Burma. Before leaving England, he wrote to the Heydons to say goodbye and thank them for their hospitality and kindness. He stayed in touch with them for many years after the war, always looking back with smile for the brief time he spent with them.

Prior to shipping off to Burma, Doug flew back to Canada for two weeks of disembarkation leave that was scheduled to end on August 22nd. Good fortune was with him, as the Japanese surrendered while he was on leave, so his posting was altered to Moncton, New Brunswick. He was officially discharged from the RCAF on October 31, 1945.

Entering civilian life after four years in the air force required some adjustments, most notably finding civilian clothes. As was the case with many things, clothing was scarce. Each veteran was given vouchers to buy one suit, along with coupons for sugar and other rationed commodities. In Canada, each veteran who held a job when he or she enlisted was guaranteed that job upon return. Rather than return to fire fighting, Doug's first thought was to return to the lumber industry in Musquodoboit. This was quickly reconsidered on the insistence of Hazel who was adamant that he pursue further education. Based on her wise counsel, he chose to enter the world of academia. Given his experience in the lumber industry, he chose to pursue forestry at the University of New Brunswick.

Beginning in 1946, he and Hazel spent four years in Fredericton where Doug attained a Bachelor's Degree in Forest Biology, graduating at the top of his class. During this time period, the pair welcomed their first child, a daughter named Sharon.

Given his high marks and his achievements as a research technician, Doug was advised to consider graduate school, which he did, enrolling at Yale University in September 1949 on a full scholarship. Remaining in Fredericton while studying, he worked as the Head of Forestry for the Maritimes and Newfoundland. He graduated with a Master of Forestry *summa cum laude*, and quickly made the decision to continue on to a doctorate degree.

While now focused on his future, his past actions did not go unnoticed. On February 9, 1950, he received, by registered mail, a Distinguished Flying Cross for his efforts during the war. The citation was simple: *"completed...numerous operations against the enemy in the course of which [he has] invariably displayed the utmost courage and devotion to duty. This navigator has completed 36 operations against targets in Germany of which eight have been against the German capital itself, and most of the others have been against distant targets where the highest standard of navigation was necessary. He has at all times remained calm and collected, even when under attack by the heaviest German defences. The assistance rendered to his captain by this combination of skill with personal courage is worthy of the highest praise, and his example to other navigators in the squadron is unsurpassed."* While Hazel had been informed by telegram from the War Department that the award had been bestowed on Doug in early 1945 while he was still flying sorties into Germany,

Doug did not learn of the honour until it arrived in registered mail five years later.

In the midst of his studies in Connecticut, Hazel presented him a bouncing baby boy, who the couple named Roderick. Having successfully graduated with a Doctorate degree, and with two young children and a wife to support, the now Dr. Redmond moved to Ottawa to begin a career with the Canadian federal government as the Deputy Minister in charge of the Forestry Service.

Once settled into Ottawa, two more children arrived, Peter and Ian. Sadly, Peter passed away at a very young age. In keeping with the stoicism that he had displayed during the war, Doug rarely spoke of the loss.

His work took him around the world as he represented Canada at the international level to spearhead the preservation of the world's forestry resources. While no longer a navigator, his air force training never left him, as he dutifully noted each flight and time in the air in his RAF log book. By the end of his life, he had flown 2,945 hours.

He would maintain that most of his travel was routine, but from time to time, incidents arose that were out of the ordinary. One of his favourite stories involved a trip to Madrid in 1966, during which a stewardess accidentally spilled a tray full of chocolate milk all over his pants. Upon arrival in London, he learned that his connecting flight was four miles from his arrival point, necessitating a quick run to make his next flight. This meant that there was no time to change clothes. When he arrived in Madrid, he found that his bags had not arrived with him. When his bags did catch up to him, he took his suit to the cleaners, who thankfully returned it to him prior to the opening ceremonies of the World Forestry Congress.

At the opening, he proudly took his place as one of Canada's senior members in a row near the world's leaders in forestry and Spain's leading politicians. He sat with his letter case full of important documents on his lap, perspiring in the warm climate. As the speeches went on, he moved the letter case to get his handkerchief. To his shock and surprise, he noted that the hair on his legs was bursting through his pants. The cleaners had somehow destroyed the synthetic material in his suit and it was rapidly disintegrating from his body heat. He quickly and deftly left the Congress and returned to the hotel before his pants completely disappeared.

Not all his experiences were so light-hearted. In 1968, while participating in an international meeting of foresters in Prague, Czechoslovakia, he awakened early one morning and was removed from the hotel. That night, the Russians had rolled into the city and deposed the government. Similarly, while acting as the senior delegate at the World Forestry Congress in Buenos Aires, the Perons made their return to Argentina. Despite the resulting chaos (bombings, crowd control using water cannons), he calmly kept his delegation safely within its hotel and secured their safe passage home. In both of these instances, the sang froid repeatedly demonstrated during the war served him well, allowing him to safely and calmly lead his fellow Canadians and members of other country's delegations through stressful and dangerous situations.

He remained with the federal government until his retirement in 1980. His work and expertise had been so highly thought of that he was awarded a lifetime achievement award by the International Union of Forest Research Officers. While significant as it was only the 13th such award of its kind at that time, it was made even more special by the fact that it was the first such award to have been granted while the recipient was still living.

Doug and Hazel Redmond celebrating their 60th Wedding Anniversary

After retirement, he spent his time with community organizations and provided advice and expertise concerning forestry related matters.

More importantly to him, though, was the opportunity to spend time with his six grandchildren and three great-grandchildren. He loved nothing more than to dote on them, and ensure that they were never in need of anything.

Active to the end, Doug passed away in Ottawa on October 29, 2008, at the age of 90.

Colin Bell

Like his navigator, Colin's actions during the Second World War were recognized with the awarding of the Distinguished Flying Cross. His courage and skills as a pilot were viewed as shining examples to which all pilots could aspire. Indeed, his unwavering devotion to the efforts of Bomber Command was evident in all of the actions that he undertook while with the squadron.

At the end of his tour, Colin volunteered for ferrying services, picking up newly built Mosquitoes from Canada and flying them via Dorval (Quebec), Goose Bay (Labrador),

Greenland, and Iceland into Prestwick, in Ayrshire, Scotland. In his view, this particular service was infinitely more difficult than flying combat missions, as the loss of planes during ferrying was horrendous. More Mosquitoes were lost crossing the Atlantic than were shot down during operations, with the added complexity of a crash in the sea around Greenland or Iceland giving a crew about 15 minutes before they would succumb to the cripplingly cold waters. In retrospect, he often said that it might have been better to volunteer for a second tour of duty with Bomber Command as a safer option.

Colin finished his RAF service in 1946 with the 162 Squadron at Blackbushe carrying diplomatic mail to various capital cities in Europe and Africa. On one occasion, Colin was tasked with flying into Vienna, a city that had been decimated in the war. Prior to the flight, he was approached by a brother officer with a request. Prior to the war, his colleague had been a student in Vienna and had been graciously taken in by a local family during his studies. His fellow officer had learned that the husband of the family had been killed on the Eastern Front and that the elderly widow and her children were trying to survive in a damaged house without heating and lighting. Wanting to repay the family for their earlier kindness and hospitality, Colin's fellow officer asked that he deliver a duffel bag full of cocoa to the family to help them survive. Never being one to shy away from helping others in need, Colin agreed to support the noble gesture.

As final preparations for departure were being made, a black car pulled up by the Mosquito and a man hurried up to speak to Colin. Identifying himself as an investigator, the man told Colin that he would be joining him on the flight in. With no passenger seating in the plane, Colin's new friend clambered into the nose cone of the former bomber and the pair took off.

Over the course of the flight, the mystery man told Colin that he was chasing after black marketeers and had been assigned to track materials in several war-torn cities. When the plane finally landed, the investigator thanked Colin for his assistance and disappeared into the night.

Colin chuckled to himself as he unloaded the duffel bag that his passenger had been lying on for the entire flight, completely unaware that he was inches from a care package for a struggling family that he might have considered as contraband.

Settling down after leaving the service,

Colin and Kathlyn - 1943

Colin and Kathlyn were blessed with the arrival of two children; Vivien and Martin. With a young family to support, he began his new career with the British public service, taking advantage of his qualifications as a Chartered Surveyor to become a Government District Valuer specializing in valuations of commercial properties. He retired from the public service in 1981.

Shortly after retirement, opportunity knocked in the form of a request from someone who felt that they were being overtaxed and who was seeking help with the valuation of his commercial property. They came to an agreement on a sum for the work and Colin heartily dug into the project. The result of his labour was a substantial reduction of the tax burden for the property holder, and a new career as an independent consultant. Beginning on what was essentially a retainer, Colin expanded his work to the point that he was able to set up his own firm, acting as the Senior Partner. Not long afterwards, he engaged his son with the firm.

In 2019, he determined that the work was becoming too complex for someone 98 years of age. The system now had too many bureaucratic regulations that produced innumerable hoops to be navigated. Realizing that failure to comply could have enormous financial consequences for his clients (consequences for which he would be liable), he chose to retire for the second time.

Sadly, prior to his retirement, Kathlyn, his beloved bride of 73 years, passed away. While understandably heartbroken, Colin chose not to wither on the vine, instead turning his attention to two areas of great interest to him: his two children, three grandchildren and four great-grandchildren; and his love for the RAF.

He now spends his time pursuing interests in touring the United Kingdom supporting the RAF Benevolent Fund through speaking engagements on Bomber Command. During his talks, he regales the audience with tales of his times in a Mosquito with his big Canadian companion, while providing compelling arguments in support of the wartime bombing campaign. For Colin, the rationale for Bomber Harris' approach has been lost over time, leading to revisionist historians painting a picture of Bomber Command as villains in the manner in which the air war was conducted.

Over the years, he has also served on the Committee of the Air Crew Association, Biggin Hill Wing, and was made a Freeman of the City of London on Jan. 13, 1987, and of the District of Huntingdonshire on Aug. 17, 2013.

In recognition of his dedication to the Royal Air Force, he was selected to participate in the 2018 Festival of Remembrance at the Royal Albert Hall, where he read the citation commemorating the 100th anniversary of the RAF. This was followed by a meeting with the Queen.

Festival of Remembrance – 2018 (Colin, third from left)

A lover of good food and wine, Colin can be found seeking both, often joining friends and colleagues at the RAF Club to share stories and laughs.

Acknowledgements

This book would not have been possible without the assistance of a number of people. Let me begin by offering my thanks to Andy Moore, an historian specializing in RAF Downham Market, who provided me with photographs and descriptions of the airbase and the town during the war years.

I would also like to acknowledge the National Archives in England, the source of the detailed operational records for the 608 Squadron, and the Bomber Command History Forum website for providing access to night raid reports that captured the actions during the period covered by this story.

My sincerest thanks to Bob Coady for his work on the cover of the book. Bob is a kindred spirit who for almost forty years has been a sounding board for many ideas, some of which might even have been good.

Special thanks also go out to Marilyn Redmond and Rod Redmond for their comments and editing of the manuscript.

In the end, this book would not be possible without the input from three important individuals. First, to Susan, my patient and supportive wife, who understood the importance of this process to me and guided me through the creative process with only the occasional boot to the rear end.

Second, I owe an immense debt of gratitude to my father's pilot, Colin Bell, who graciously welcomed me into his home and shared his wartime remembrances (and a few drinks) so that I might have a more complete understanding of my father's life during the war, the world of Bomber Command and the lives of an RAF base.

Third, and finally, my love and admiration for my father, Douglas Redmond, who shared glimpses of his military experiences, taught me to be a caring and thoughtful human being, and instilled in me a passion for the written word.

Annex 1

Colin Bell and Doug Redmond's Operations

Date	Hour	Details	Flying Time
Training Flights			
24/08/44	11:25	Familiarization – carried eight bombs	2:20
25/08/44	09:30	Cross country flight to get GEE fixes	3:20
25/08/44	20:50	Test flight	0:20
25/08/44	21:20	Test flight	0:20
26/08/44	11:15	Cross country GEE and Dead Reckoning (DR) exercise	3:35
27/08/44	17:40	Night Flying Test (NFT)	1:10
27/08/44	22:00	Cross country GEE and DR exercise, with four bombs	3:50
28/08/44	18:35	NFT with four bombs	0:45
28/08/44	22:30	Cross country GEE and DR exercise, with four bombs	3:40
29/08/44	19:55	NFT	0:15

Date	Time	Mission	Duration
29/08/44	22:10	Cross country GEE and DR exercise	3:45
30/08/44	15:05	Cross country GEE and DR exercise	1:45

Combat

Date	Time	Mission	Duration
05/09/44	23:10	Hannover – 4 x 500 lb bombs – photo	4:15
06/09/44	20:45	Hamburg – 4 x 500	3:35
08/09/44	20:45	Nurnberg – 4 x 500	4:35
09/09/44	21:20	Brunswick – 4 x 500 – photo	3:30
11/09/44	21:35	Berlin - 4 x 500	4:35
12/09/44	21:45	Berlin - 4 x 500 – photo	4:40
15/09/44	23:45	Berlin – 4 x 500 – photo	4:35
02/10/44	18:50	Brunswick – 4 x 500 – photo	3:35
05/10/44	18:05	Saarbrucken – 4 x 500	3:40
06/10/44	17:40	Berlin – 4 x 500	4:55
10/10/44	18:15	Cologne - 4 x 500	2:50
14/10/44	03:55	Cologne - 4 x 500	2:55
14/10/44	23:50	Ludwigshafen – 4 x 500	4:05
16/10/44	22:45	Cologne - 4 x 500	3:00
23/10/44	17:10	Berlin – 4 x 500	4:15
27/10/44	20:40	Berlin – 1 x 500	4:30
29/10/44	18:05	Cologne - 4 x 500	3:05
31/10/44	18:30	Hamburg – 4 x 500	3:35
02/11/44	16:50	Osnabruck – 4 x 500 – photo	4:00
03/11/44	23:55	Berlin – 4 x 500 – photo	4:30
05/11/44	18:10	Stuttgart - 4 x 500 – photo	4:30

Bloody Terrified

09/11/44	02:00	Hannover – pilot's oxygen failed (hypoxia) – turned back	2:10
21/11/44	02:30	Hannover – starboard engine unserviceable	0:15
21/11/44	16:55	Castrop Rauxel – 4 x 500	3:20
23/11/44	16:55	Hannover – 4 x 500	3:15
25/11/44	21:45	Nurnberg – 4 x 500 – photo	4:20
28/11/44	17:10	Nurnberg – 4 x 500 – photo	4:50
29/11/44	19:00	Hannover – 4 x 500 – photo	3:50
30/11/44	10:15	Duisberg – 4 x 500	3:55
02/12/44	19:05	Hagen – 4 x 500	3:30
05/12/44	19:20	Nurnberg – 4 x 500 – photo	4:20
08/12/44	12:45	Duisberg – 4 x 500 – photo – diverted to Upwood	3:40
11/12/44	17:05	Hannover – 4 x 500 – diverted to Wyton	3:50
16/12/44	17:20	Weisbaden – recalled	0:25
28/12/44	16:30	Franfurt – 4 x 500 – photo	4:05
30/12/44	16:40	Hannover – 4 x 500 – photo	3:30
01/01/45	16:15	Hanau – 4 x 500 – photo	4:10
07/01/45	20:40	Hannover – 4 x 500	3:15
14/01/45	17:55	Berlin – 4 x 500 – photo – diverted to Wyton	5:05
18/01/45	03:10	Magdeburg – 4 x 500 – photo	3:50
21/01/45	18:40	Kassel – 4 x 500 – photo	3:40
22/01/45	16:55	Hannover – 4 x 500	3:45
28/01/45	18:05	Berlin – 4 x 500	4:15

10/02/45	21:50	Hannover – 4 x 500	3:20
14/02/45	19:45	Magdeburg – 4 x 500	3:45
19/02/45	17:55	Erfurt – 4 x 500 – photo – FIDO landing	4:05
21/02/45	18:40	Berlin – 4 x 500 – photo	4:15
22/02/45	18:00	Berlin – 4 x 500 – photo	4:30
24/02/45	18:05	Neuss – 4 x 500 – photo	3:30
25/02/45	18:30	Erfurt – port engine failure – diverted to Woodbridge	1:00
26/02/45	18:35	Berlin – 4 x 500 – photo	4:30
29/02/45	18:05	Munich – 4 x 500	4:30
01/03/45	19:35	Berlin – 3 x 500 – 1 Target Indicator	5:00
03/03/45	18:15	Berlin – 4 x 500 – photo	4:10

Annex 2

608 Squadron Losses from September 1944 to March 1945

September 13/14, 1944
Mosquito XX KB359
On an operation to Berlin, crashed near Naven with the loss of both crew members.
Squadron Leader C.R. Barrett, DFC, RAFVR (veteran of over 60 missions)
Flying Officer E.S. Fogden, RAFVR

September 15/16, 1944
Mosquito XX KB239
On an operation to Berlin, crashed at Bahnof with the loss of both crew members.
Flight Lieutenant B.H. Smith, RCAF
Sergeant L.F. Pegg, RAFVR

October 9, 1944
Mosquito XX KB261
On an operation to Wilhemshaven, crashed on return to base with loss of both crew members.
Flight Lieutenant R.G. Gardner, RAFVR
Flying Officer O.C. Sweetman, DFM RAFVR

October 11/12, 1944
Mosquito XX KB348
On an operation to Berlin, with the loss of both crew members.
Flying Officer S.W. Reeder, RAFVR
First Sergeant R.J. Bolton, RAAF

November 6/7, 1944
Mosquito XX KB364
The aircraft crashed at Bawdeswell, near Norwich, with the loss of both crew members.
Pilot Officer J. McLean
Sergeant M.L. Tansley, RAFVR

November 10/11, 1944
Mosquito XX KB360
On a mission to Hanover, crashed near Wisbeach with the loss of the pilot.
Flight Lieutenant S.D. Webb, RCAF
Flying Officer Campbell was injured but survived.

December 6/7, 1944
Mosquito XX KB235
On an operation to Berlin, crashed near Wijhe, in Holland, with the loss of both crew members.
Flying Officer G.R.E. Weir, RAFVR
Flying Officer J/E.C. Hardy, RAFVR

February 23/24, 1945
Mosquito XX KB350
On an operation to Berlin, lost without a trace.
Flying Officer R.A.A. Doherty, RAF
Flying Officer L. Moore, RAF

Annex 3

Resources

BOOKS

Bishop, Edward. *Mosquito - Wooden Wonder.* New York, Ballantine Books Inc., July, 1971.

Blunt, Barry. *608 Mosquito Bomber Squadron.* Barry Blunt, Stockport, United Kingdom, March, 2001.

Bowyer, Chaz. *Path Finders at War.* Shepperton, Surrey, Ian Allan Ltd., 1977.

Chorley, W R. *Royal Air Force Bomber Command Losses of the Second World War 1945.* Hersham, Surrey, Midland Publishing, 1998.

Frankland, Noble. *Bomber Offensive. The Devastation of Europe.* New York, Ballantine Books Inc., April, 1970.

Hilling, John B. *Strike Hard. A Bomber Airfield at War. RAF Downham Market and Its Squadrons 1942-46.* Allan Sutton Publishing Limited, 1995.

Hogg, Ian V. *The Guns 1939-45.* New York, Ballantine Books Inc., April, 1970.

Holliday, Joe. *Mosquito! The Wooden Wonder Aircraft of World War II.* Toronto, Ontario, Doubleday Canada, Limited, 1970.

McIntosh, Dave. *Terror in the Starboard Seat.* Markham, Ontario, Paperjacks Ltd., December, 1981.

Partridge, Eric. *A Dictionary of RAF Slang.* Penguin Random House UK, 1945.

Price, Albert. *Luftwaffe.* New York, Ballantine Books Inc., February, 1970.

Smith, Albert and Ian. *Mosquito Pathfinder. A Navigator's 90 WWII Bomber Operations.* Manchester, United Kingdom, Crécy Publishing Limited, 2003.

RECORDINGS

Harris, Sir Arthur. *Address to the RAF Club.* 1984.

Ian Redmond

Printed in Great Britain
by Amazon